THE
FILMS
OF
W.C. FIELDS

THE FILMS
OF
W.C. FIELDS

by Donald Deschner

Introduction
by
Arthur Knight

The Citadel Press

Secaucus, New Jersey

Fourth paperbound edition, 1971
Copyright © 1966 by Donald Deschner
All rights reserved
Published by Citadel Press, Inc.
A subsidiary of Lyle Stuart, Inc.
120 Enterprise Ave., Secaucus, N. J. 07094
In Canada: George J. McLeod Limited
73 Bathurst St., Toronto 2B, Ontario
Manufactured in the United States of America
Designed by Martin Fuller
ISBN 0-8065-0143-X

CONTENTS

Introduction   *Arthur Knight*   17
Biography   19
Speaking of Benefits   *W. C. Fields*   26
Anything for a Laugh   *W. C. Fields*   29

THE FILMS

Pool Sharks   35
Janice Meredith   36
Sally of the Sawdust   38
That Royle Girl   41
It's the Old Army Game   44
So's Your Old Man   47
The Potters   50
Running Wild   53
Two Flaming Youths   56
Tillie's Punctured Romance   59
Fools for Luck   62
The Golf Specialist   64
Her Majesty Love   65
Million Dollar Legs   69

If I Had a Million   72
Four Mack Sennet Shorts   76
International House   80
Tillie and Gus   83
Alice in Wonderland   86
Six of a Kind   89
You're Telling Me   93
The Old-Fashioned Way   95
Mrs. Wiggs of the Cabbage Patch   99
It's a Gift   103
David Copperfield   106
Mississippi   112
The Man on the Flying Trapeze   117
Poppy   121
The Big Broadcast of 1938   128
You Can't Cheat an Honest Man   134
My Little Chickadee   140
Bank Dick   148
Never Give a Sucker an Even Break   154
Tales of Manhattan   162
Follow the Boys   164
Song of the Open Road   170
Sensations of 1945   174

The Old-Fashioned Way   *Otis Ferguson*   180
W. C. Fields and the Cosmos   *Heywood Broun*   184

Index   191

ACKNOWLEDGEMENTS

Grateful acknowledgement is made to the many individuals and organizations who aided the author in the preparation of this book.

I especially want to thank Universal Studios; Paramount Pictures; the Rank Organization; the Larry Edmunds Book Store; Ray Stuart; Dorothy Crawford and the Crawford Theatre Collection at Yale University; William Crain and the Hoblitzelle Theatre Arts Library at the University of Texas; Joseph Longo and the Museum of Modern Art; Mr. and Mrs. Hampton and the Silent Movie Theatre, Los Angeles; The Los Angeles Public Library; Jimmy Starr; Bruco Enterprises; Les Adams; United Press International; Scholastic Magazines, Inc.; *The Times* (London); *The New York Times*; *Time*; *Newsweek*; *The New Republic*; *The Nation*; Dorothy Chamberlain; Twyman Films, Inc.; Gene Ringgold; Cliff McCarty; Lillian Schwartz and the staff of the Motion Picture Academy of Arts and Sciences; Bettman Archive, Inc.; William Fowler; the Directors' Guild of America; the Screen Actors' Guild; Ray Thelan; the Collector's Book Shop; Robert Pike; Movie Star News; H. Kier; Morris T. Johnson; the Hollywood *Citizen-News*; *The Commonweal*; Culver Pictures, Inc.; and Harvey Stewart.

If there was ever a great clown in this time of changeover from beer and music hall to the universal distribution of radio and films, I would say it was in the person and the character and the undying, if corny, gusto of Bill Fields, who moved mountains until they fell on him, and then brushed himself off and looked around for more.

Otis Ferguson
The New Republic
November 10, 1941

The impediment to a sober appraisal of a master buffoon like W.C. Fields resides in the reviewer's self-administered compulsion to be ponderously witty in his discussion of the comedian's work. Let us drop the elephantine irony this morning and approach a great man with becoming humility and awe. Since it is the function of the funny man to massage the tortured ego of his auditors by showing himself to be even more witless and sub-human in his deportment than they are in theirs, it is natural for his hearers to adopt toward him a falsely inflated sense of superiority. Thus the clown fulfills his divine mission at the moment that his public regards him with amused aloofness. Mr. Fields is a great comedian because he traffics in high and cosmic matters relating to man's eternal helplessness, frustration and defeat. It is a fitting tribute to his eminence that most of the filmgoers who are privileged to observe him are content to laugh at his brilliantly conceived and subtly executed jocosities. A few, sensing the parable of man's eternal disillusion which Mr. Fields manages to suggest even when he is most painfully lunatic, are sometimes a little sad in the midst of their laughter, knowing suddenly that they are mocking themselves. Not to be aware of the tragic overtones in the work of this middle-aged, whiskey-nosed, fumbling and wistfully incompetent gentleman is to be ignorant of the same tragic overtones in the comedy of Don Quixote de la Mancha. To be of the belief that Mr. Fields is no more than a funny man is to hold the opinion that *Gulliver's Travels* is a book for children.

André Sennwald
The New York Times,
January 13, 1935

The world of W.C. Fields was a planet all of its own. For
him, inanimate objects seemed to have a life and will all
their own. He made the best of a bad business; what is
easy for us—picking up a bag of golf clubs or moving a
chair—was horribly difficult for him. Small children, sus-
penders, dress shirts, ties, cigar boxes, bass fiddles, tele-
phones, foods—all were his sworn enemies. He moved
through the world with a feeling of wariness for his sur-
roundings and a hastily assumed air of nonchalance, con-
fident that he would in the end prevail.

Alan P. Twyman
Twyman Films, Inc.

THE
FILMS
OF
W.C. FIELDS

INTRODUCTION

by Arthur Knight

Comedians have never been the happiest of men. No small part of their appeal is the wry or jaundiced eye with which they view the world and its ways, pointing up with savage or what passes for affectionate humor the follies of their fellowmen. Theirs is no lovers' quarrel: Jokes are their armor in a never-ending war against stupidity, convention, prejudice, or merely the opposite sex; gags are their scarcely camouflaged weapons of counter-attack. Of all the great comedians, however, none has ever been more openly hostile, more flagrantly misanthropic, more downright cantankerous than William Claude Dukenfield, better known as W. C. Fields. Perhaps it is not true that he hated the entire world, although in his later years he exhibited a deeply ingrained suspicion of every person and institution he encountered in it. Nevertheless, his running feud with Baby LeRoy, his in-instinctive distrust of all banks (and bankers), and his snarling belligerence in the face of authority, on-screen or off, are all too indicative of his basic attitudes. "Any man who hates small dogs and children can't be *all* bad" is more than a bit of Fieldsian humor. It is a primary tenet of his philosophy.

The reasons are not far to seek. When Fields was growing up, in his native Philadelphia, neither small dogs nor children were particularly kind to him. His own childhood was almost spectacularly unhappy—so much so that when he was eleven he hit his father over the head with a shovel and ran away from home, never to return. Early hardships after that were so varied and poignant that they might have been torn from the pages of Charles Dickens or Horatio Alger. The famous nose, for example, did not derive from his well-known affection for the bottle, but from a drubbing he received when a bunch of kids ganged up on him during his vagrant years. And

the affection for the bottle also came from the lean times, when a free lunch could be gobbled with a nickel glass of beer. What differentiates Fields from the typical Dickens or Alger hero, however, although all eventually made it to the top, is that Fields never attained their manufactured magnanimity of spirit. At nine he had set himself the shimmering goal of becoming the world's greatest juggler, and he practiced at it until his fingers bled. Once he had mastered that intricate art, he began the climb from fair grounds to burlesque, from vaudeville to Ziegfeld revues and on to the movies; but always he was being mulcted by agents, managers and partners. By the time he arrived, through the not so simple expedient of adding his inimitably orotund comedy patter to his insuperable juggling skill, he had learned to trust no one, and had long since begun his unique system of savings, stashing away small amounts of "getaway money" under assumed names in banks all over the country. For him, the most unsettling sight in the world was a bank teller with a hat on—a promise of imminent departure that Fields later incorporated into one of his best films, *The Bank Dick.*

Small wonder, then, that W. C. Fields was never a lovable clown. He snarled and grumbled and flailed out with his stick at the slightest provocation—and particularly if the provokers were smaller than he. He was a bully, a braggart, a chaser and a lush. He was cowardly, mean, larcenous and a liar. He was, in short, the very antonym of every Boy Scout virtue. And one was never quite certain where the screen character ended and the real Fields took over. The actor Thomas Mitchell often liked to recall a visit that he paid his old friend in a sanatorium shortly before his death. He found Fields engaged in the by no means habitual pastime of

With Charlie McCarthy

thumbing through a Bible. When Mitchell asked what he was doing, Fields looked up and muttered, "Looking for loopholes." He probably found some, too.

But if Fields had none of the pathos of such classic comic figures as Chaplin, Keaton or Langdon, his on-screen character provided numerous areas of identification for the common man. He was the eternally henpecked husband, nagged not only by wife and mother-in-law, but by his smart-alecky kids as well. Let him try to play golf, and sticky paper promptly wound itself around his club. A snooze on the back porch was turned into a nightmare by the milkman, the telephone, an insurance salesman, and the brat upstairs. When he ran a drug-store, his big sale was a two-cent stamp—and his irate patron insisted on having the one in the center of the sheet. In other words, he was constantly being put upon

by friends, foes and Fate—a form of mild paranoia that most of us share to some degree. What made it all so amusing with Fields was his flamboyant braggadocio until the chips were down. Comedy has been defined as tragedy that happens to somebody else; the jest is improved when that somebody else is a good deal less than amiable.

A similar mechanism surmounts his obvious fraudulence. In innumerable films Fields played a con man, a bunko artist, or a card shark. In *Poppy* he sold a spurious talking dog to a bartender; no sooner was the deal completed than he had the dog say, "Just for that, I'll never talk again." "Stubborn little fellow," observed Fields, beating a hasty retreat, "he probably means it, too." In another film, he manipulates the old shell game to his profit, meanwhile reminding the suckers, "You can't cheat an honest man." But invariably in all his films his fraudulence would be exposed, his bluff called. There is a delicious moment in *Mississippi* when, playing a game of five-card draw poker, he finds to his delight that he has dealt himself four aces. Then comes the tremor when he discovers that his fifth card is also an ace. He tosses it aside and draws—another ace. He uses every subterfuge he can summon to rid himself of the offending card, but every new one that he smuggles into his hand is also an ace. Eventually, one of his table-mates calls, setting a pistol on the green baize at the same time. "Oh, just a little old pair," says Fields, hastily folding his cards, "I'm afraid I was only bluffing." Breathes there a man with soul so dead that he has never enjoyed seeing a con man get his comeuppance? Fields had mastered the art of being insincere in earnest.

More fundamental than any of this, however, is the fact that on films Fields was forever acting out his own hostilities against the world that had so sorely wounded him in his youth. Significantly, he wrote his own scripts (often under such fanciful sobriquets at Otis J. Cribblecoblis or Mahatma Kane Jeeves), and thus was able to incorporate into them his many private vengeances. His plots abound with rascally bankers, idiot producers and pushy salesmen. Road hogs happened to be his pet peeve at the moment he was asked to appear in *If I Had a Million*; typically, his filmic revenge was to buy up a used car lot and charge his battered wrecks against every faulty driver who crossed his path.

The wonderful thing was that no sooner did Fields begin to work out his own aggressions on film than audiences everywhere recognized that in fact these were their aggressions, too. They too were henpecked. They too were being cheated. The cards were always stacked against them, too. They loved the unlovable Fields empathically because they understood that in his funny, twisted, implacable way, he was eternally fighting the same enemies they were. Many a man has been elected President for less. For Fields, it was enough to be the not-so-loyal, but ever-present opposition.

BIOGRAPHY

In the late 1870's James Dukenfield, a Cockney, emigrated with his parents to the United States. Some time after settling in Philadelphia, he met and married Kate Felton. Their first child, William Claude Dukenfield, was probably born in January, 1879, although no records exist to verify this. In the following ten years the Dukenfields had four more children, Le Roy, Walter, Elsie Mae, and Adele. The family was poor, and the father made his living by selling vegetables and fruit from a horse-drawn cart. William attended school for about four years and then worked with his father. But his mind was not always on his work, and as a result father and son were often at odds. Shortly after his eleventh birthday the two had a fight that lasted for days, and at one point father hit son over the head with a shovel handle. It is no wonder that a few days later William left home and did not see any of his family for several years.

For the next few years, Fields lived as best he could, first in a hole in the ground where he and neighbor children had often played. Friends brought him food at first. Soon, however, he was on his own and had to steal food and clothing to survive. Businessmen who came to know him chased him from their establishments. He was beaten a few times and spent many a night in jail. Finally he moved into a corner of a blacksmith's shop where he could stay warm through the winter. His voice was changing, and it hardened with the rasp it would have for the rest of his lifetime. His sensitivity to his hardships created fears that would disturb him in later years. But luckily at this time he also carefully studied the game of pool, acquiring a skill he would someday use to perform a great comic routine.

Then he got a job helping to deliver ice. He seemed to enjoy the work, although he had to be at work by three in the morning. The boss was kind enough in dividing the work to give the easier to William. They would make deliveries until about noon, when they would stop for a free lunch at one of the establishments that bought ice from them. And Fields was able to save money, since his weekly salary was $3.00 and his monthly rent for an attic apartment was only $5.00. Many of his pleasures were free. But he did not waste his time. Most of the afternoons

With his father in Paris   UNIVERSITY OF TEXAS

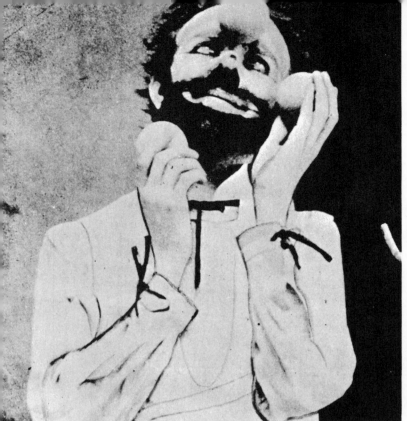

An early photo of his juggling act

A very early picture

he spent developing his skills in juggling, which were highly developed for a lad of thirteen.

Next spring he read a notice of the opening of Plymouth Park, an amusement park near Norristown, Pa. Performers were needed. Fields applied and was hired. Most of his material had been borrowed from the acts of other performers, such as the Byrne Brothers, whom he very much admired. He began to develop the stunt of pretending to lose the items he was juggling and then catch them as if in a last-minute rescue. It always drew applause, and he played variations on it as long as he juggled.

He did well at the Park. During the late summer he was on the same bill with an Austrian teeterboard act which had plans to go on to Atlantic City. He decided to go with them. A few days before he left, Fields had a benefit for himself, which everyone else seemed to enjoy and out of which he collected well over a hundred dollars to help defray the costs of his trip.

A few weeks later (in 1893) he was in Atlantic City. The management at Fortescue's Pier was doubtful of his talents when they looked at the young boy in his ragged clothes. However, Billy Watson saw the act and suggested they hire the lad. His salary rose to ten dollars a week, but he actually had two jobs to perform. The first was his juggling act, which he repeated several times during the day and evening. The second job was his "drownings." Whenever business was slow, he had to swim out into the ocean and cry for help. The lifeguards would then rescue him. These "drownings," it was hoped, would attract a crowd, which would then spend some money on the various amusements and shows. It was rough, exhausting work for a young lad, and it was not long before Fields

left his employer and went to work for a competitor. He worked only a few weeks in Atlantic City for the new company before he was placed in a road company. It was his first tour and he saw many new acts to copy. However, in the middle of the winter, the manager of the company disappeared with all the funds, leaving everyone stranded in Kent, Ohio, without their weekly salaries. A railroad agent befriended Fields and lent him some

On a vaudeville tour about 1903

money to return east. In later years Fields recalled the incident as one of the few kindnesses he had met in his teens.

Back in New Jersey, he worked for a circus in a variety of menial tasks, from drummer to elephant waterboy. Finally, though with some doubt, he returned to the company that had left him stranded and went out on the road again for them, but this time with more success. When he returned to New York he found an opening for his act at the Globe Museum on Third Avenue. An impresario who saw his act offered Fields more money to join his traveling company. Fields accepted the offer of Jim Fulton and soon left for the midwest. For the first time, reporters and audiences took special notice of Fields' acts. Fred Irwin, who at that time had the highest prestige for his circuit of shows and performers, was interested in hiring Fields. When the boy asked for thirty-five dollars a week, Irwin was outraged; but when Fields waved the newspaper clippings in his face, Irwin agreed to pay the price. Some months later, with a new batch of newspaper clippings, Fields made Irwin raise his salary to seventy-five dollars a week. Irwin called him a bandit, but paid the salary.

After eight years, William finally wrote a letter to his family, enclosing some money for his mother. That was in December of 1898, and his days of want were finally over. There were more tours across the country for Fields as vaudeville grew into a popular entertainment. At the age of nineteen, he was billed as "The Distinguished Comedian" and was receiving one hundred and twenty-five dollars a week. About this time he began his curious but explainable habit of opening a savings account in a bank in every city and town in which he played. He had to satisfy himself that he need never be stranded in a strange city again without money, anywhere in the world. In spite of his distrust of banks, a robbery that occurred in San Francisco convinced him that entrusting his money to their vaults was safer than carrying it on his person. At one point in his later career he reputedly had over seven hundred accounts around the world. Many of these accounts were opened under fictitious names, and some of the uninvestigated accounts may still to this day be languishing in banks.

In 1901 Fields, who was in his early twenties, was offered his first foreign tour. He opened at the Palace in London. During one of Fields' London runs, King Edward VII visited the show in which he was appearing. It was such a hit that the King visited William backstage and invited him to Buckingham Palace to perform for a gala function. Fields of course was surprised and pleased. He was even more astonished when only one other performer appeared that night for the King and his guests. The other guest performer was a French actress, who recited passages from a play by Rostand called *L'Aiglon*. Her name was Sarah Bernhardt. Then Fields presented several of his comic acts. The guests were very enthusiastic in showing their appreciation for both performers.

The European tours added to his self-confidence, and developed him into a world personality. When Fields appeared as a star with top billing at the Folies-Bergere, a young Englishman appeared on the same program— Charles Chaplin, just starting his career. Maurice Chevalier also appeared on this program. Later Fields traveled to South Africa, and while playing there he met two American cowboys: Will Rogers, selling horses; and Tom Mix, who had come for "some excitement."

Back from overseas, W.C. Fields met and married Miss Harriet Hughes of New York. She was a dancer in the show he was working in at the time. Part of the honeymoon included a few weeks in Philadelphia for the first visit to his family since he left home. Everyone got along

In the Ziegfeld Follies of 1919   UNIVERSITY OF TEXAS

surprisingly well and enjoyed the visit. Fields impressed his family and neighbors with tales of his travels.

A year later, when he went on another European tour, he took his wife and one of his brothers with him. These trips now became a regular feature of his life. He planned to tour about half the year outside the country and about half the year in the United States.

A few years later, Fields joined a company producing a new play called *The Ham Tree*. Even though it was a show with a superficial story line into which were fitted numerous available acts, this was Fields' first play. He stayed with the show throughout its New York run and then went on the road with it for the tour of 1906-7. It was one of the big commercial successes of the time.

When the play closed, he returned to regular vaudeville and continued traveling widely. Shortly before the war he was making one thousand dollars a week by playing two shows a night for two different companies. A regular show was played at the Palace in downtown New York, and then he hurried to do a late show at the uptown Alhambra.

W.C. Fields was on the road in Australia when World War I broke out. He received a telegram from the New York producer Charles Dillingham, who asked him to return immediately for a speaking part in a new play, *Watch Your Step*. Because of German submarines in the Pacific, Fields had difficulty finding a ship that would sail, but one courageous captain was sailing his freighter to San Francisco and Fields got passage on it. In New

was being carefully banked, for he had a frightening feeling that he was headed for a fall. However, it never came. When he left the *Follies*, he played for one year in the *George White's Scandals*.

The next play was to be his greatest show, and in it he found a role he would twice repeat on film. On September 3, 1923, *Poppy* opened at the New Apollo Theater in New York City, with W.C. Fields playing the lead. The musical comedy was written by Dorothy Donnelly, with music by Steven Jones and Arthur Samuels. and produced by Philip Goodman. Actually, Fields helped rewrite parts of the show, a habit he would take with him when he went into film-making. He lovingly played the role of Eustace McGargle, a gypsy rogue who milked the crowds attending country fairs. Madge Kennedy co-starred, playing his young daughter. The play was a hit. Critics like Heywood Broun applauded the show and its performers. *Poppy* ran for more than a year and Fields was the toast of the theatrical season.

Before the play closed, Fields played a character part as a drunken British soldier in a big historical-costume picture called *Janice Meredith*, which starred Marion Davies. But his first important film was to be made in 1925 on Long Island. D.W. Griffith was hired to direct

In the Ziegfeld Follies of 1922   UNIVERSITY OF TEXAS

York he was given the part, joining the show a few days before it opened. But the day after the show opened, his act was cut out of it. Luckily, Gene Buck, Ziegfeld's close aide, had seen Fields in the new show, had liked his work, and had told him to come to his office when he left the show. Fields hesitated a few days, then went to see Buck, and was hired to join the *Ziegfeld Follies of 1915* for a weekly salary of two hundred dollars. Fields was now at the top of the theatrical world. However, Ziegfeld thought comedians only a necessary evil in his *Follies*, and he and Fields had occasional arguments over the form and content of certain acts.

In 1915 W.C. Fields made his first movie. Called *Pool Sharks*, it was a short incorporating the principal gags from his famous pool act. It was made by the British Gaumont Company in New York.

Fields appeared in every version of the *Ziegfeld Follies* from 1915 through 1921. His salary rose during this time to over one thousand dollars a week. Most of the money

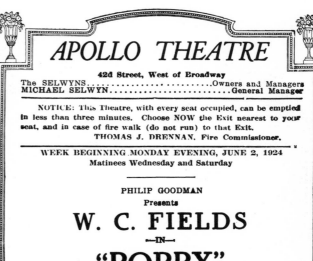

APOLLO THEATRE

42d Street, West of Broadway

The SELWYNS............................Owners and Managers
MICHAEL SELWYN........................General Manager

NOTICE: This Theatre, with every seat occupied, can be emptied in less than three minutes. Choose NOW the Exit nearest to your seat, and in case of fire walk (do not run) to that Exit.
THOMAS J. DRENNAN. Fire Commissioner.

WEEK BEGINNING MONDAY EVENING, JUNE 2, 1924
Matinees Wednesday and Saturday

PHILIP GOODMAN
Presents

W. C. FIELDS
—IN—

"POPPY"

A New Musical Comedy in Three Acts
Book and Lyrics by Dorothy Donnelly
Music by Stephen Jones and Arthur Samuels
Staged by the Author and Philip Goodman
Musical Numbers Staged by Julian Alfred
Settings Designed by Ralph Barton
Costumes Designed by Charles Le Maire
Orchestra Under Direction of Gus Salzer
Entire Orchestration by Stephen Jones

PROGRAM CONTINUED ON SECOND PAGE FOLLOWING

The Cast

(As the Characters Appear)

Sarah Tucker..........................Isabelle Winlocke
Shorty, A Peanut Vendor................William Blanche
Amos Sniffen..........................John Cherry
Mary Delafield........................Luella Gear
William Van Wyck......................Alan Edwards
Princess Vronski Mameluke Pasha Tubbs..........Emma Janvier
Mortimer Pottle.......................Jerry Delaney
Prof. Eustace McGargle................W. C. Fields
Poppy McGargle........................Victoria White
Judge Delafield.......................Hugh Chilvers
Premier Dancer........................Marion Chambers
Special Dancers.......Hilda Burt, Gladys Reith, Violet Vale,
.. and Devah Worrell

A page of the program for Poppy   UNIVERSITY OF TEXAS

Magikie Theat.
Boston Mass.
Dear Friend Harry :— Aug 30/24

many thanks for your kind letter with enclosed "snap shot" which arrived to-day. The 'snaps' were so fine & clear— I was so glad to see you again, and to find you looking so well and happy. I forgot to tell you how much I enjoyed reading your book The Unmasking of Robert Houdin.

It reminded me to send stamp out for your latest which I hear is even better.

With best compliments to your good Photographer and all good wish for continued success health & happiness for yourself—

As Ever—
Bill Fields

P.S. I am having the snaps enlarged

A letter to Harry Houdini
UNIVERSITY OF TEXAS

the film version of *Poppy* for Paramount. Carol Dempster was to play Fields' daughter, and her part was enlarged for the film, while a futile attempt was made by the studio to reduce Fields' part. For some unknown reason the title of the film was changed from *Poppy* to *Sally of the Sawdust*, and United Artists distributed it. It was not one of Griffith's better films and, although somewhat successful, it did not fulfill the studio's expectations. Griffith

hired Fields for his next film, *That Royle Girl*, in an effort to save the film, but Fields' part was not in keeping with the rest of the film, and only weakened the film more.

W.C. Fields' first film, *Pool Sharks*, was made when he was thirty-six, and in the thirty-one remaining years of his life he would make more than thirty-three features and several short films. His early films fluctuated from good to bad, from popular to unsuccessful, but he kept making film after film, often as many as three in one year. Most of his films were made for Paramount, and several were announced that were never made. In the mid-twenties Fields moved to California to make movies on the West Coast.

In later years he would complain of the money he lost in the crash of the stock market in 1929. Although through the years this account became more and more exaggerated in the telling, it is true that Fields had placed his trust in a New York banker, who was responsible for his loss. It was the last time Fields would trust anyone who wanted to talk about investments. The loss of the cash was not as painful as the loss of pride that Fields felt when he discovered he had trusted an unscrupulous banker.

W.C. Fields settled permanently at Toluca Lake, near Burbank, Calif. Here he had a mansion with large grounds sloping down to the lake. During the thirties he made sixteen films, ranging in subject matter from stand-

With director Edward Sutherland and Jack Oakie, watching the filming of a scene from Poppy

With Shirley Ross in 1938   *At his ranch in California*

ard classics like *Alice in Wonderland* and *David Copperfield*, to a musical with Bing Crosby and Joan Bennett called *Mississippi*, to an all-star extravaganza, *The Big Broadcast of 1938*.

Fields often interjected his own material into films. One gag that finally found its way onto the film after several arguments over its use, was a scene in which Fields shoots the picture tube of a television set to pieces because he can't stand the crooner appearing on the screen. The gag appeared in *International House*, and Rudy Vallee, who was the victim of the joke, was not sure it should be permitted. At other times, Fields was not successful in adding his own material, but he kept the directors on their toes.

In the mid-thirties the first of several annoying illnesses came upon Fields. He spent several months at Seboba Hot Springs, near Riverside, Calif. And for some weeks he was in the Riverside Hospital with pneumonia.

It was during one of his illnesses that he recorded a short piece for a radio show honoring Adolph Zukor. In this way, he found a new entertainment medium and was soon appearing with Edgar Bergen and Charlie McCarthy on the "Chase and Sanborn Hour," with a beginning salary of sixty-five hundred dollars a week. Audiences enjoyed the tug of war between W.C. Fields and Charlie McCarthy over the air, little realizing that much of the dialogue was being created on the spot by Fields. Only an experienced performer like Edgar Bergen could have kept pace with the sudden introduction of an entirely new script. The advertisers were often on the edge of their seats waiting for Fields to go too far. Two years later he moved to another sponsor, Lucky Strike cigarettes. Again he ran into trouble with his satiric jabs at advertisers and anyone else he might take a dislike to.

In the late thirties Fields left Paramount and went to Universal where, with Lester Cowan's help, he was to make his greatest films. He was free at last to make the films he wished to make. Written principally by Fields, these films became almost monologues for the comedian. *Bank Dick* and *Never Give a Sucker an Even Break* were indeed displays of everything W.C. Fields was and wanted to be. Then illness again prevented him from working regularly. In 1944 he made guest appearances in three films. In one of these, *Follow the Boys*, he performed his pool act, much as he had performed it in his first film in 1915. On Christmas Day, 1946, Fields died in Pasadena, California.

SPEAKING OF BENEFITS

by W.C.Fields

There may be a heartier laugh in other things, but I doubt it. For me the jolliest moment in life is when the frank friend says:

"Gee, what an easy life. Just eight performances a week and that's all."

The same vest that expands and contracts with merriment as I roar at this wisecrack probably contains my notations of the benefits I'm scheduled to play in the ensuing day or two. Sometimes, as I look the list over, I really begin to doubt whether I'm going to be able to keep my engagement at the theatre each evening.

They're all for a worthy cause, of course, and I feel sure that some of them are. There are those, however, that serve merely for the glorification of the lad that's arranging them, and unfortunately it's hard to separate the sheep from the goats. In fact, quite often I've been the goat.

I'm old enough to know better, to be sure, but I don't. There was the time, when I was playing vaudeville in Johannesburg, South Africa. The Governor General—Lord Maulder, I think—sent around word that his children were having a party the next day at Governor's House and would I stage a few choice juggles for their benefit.

Of course, I would. I didn't particularly want to, but I would. A Governor General is a Governor General, particularly in South Africa.

For twenty minutes the next afternoon I stood in a pouring rain outside the Governor's house, loaded down with cigar boxes, golf clubs, and rubber balls, while a platoon of footmen debated whether I ought to be allowed to enter. Finally, I was told the Governor General was busy, but that I could go ahead and amuse the children.

I amused them my very best for thirty minutes. I had a running refrain of "Wo'ts 'E Do That For?" to help me along and the cunning little tykes were only too willing, whenever I purposely dropped a prop in the mis-

taken notion that I was planting an effect, to pick it up and gum my trick for me. But even that half-hour came to an end.

Three seconds before its end the Governor General himself appeared. And so I was privileged to do my bit all over again. The kiddies had learned the routine pretty well by this time and so there was a lot of innocent merriment, you may be sure, every time they crabbed my act. When it was all over, I was allowed to go out in the rain again and without a fine or anything.

To get back to the question of benefits, they're all associated in my mind with a sentence that I'll never forget. In fact, if any actor wants to earn an undying name for applause, just let him step forward at the next Lambs Gambol and say:

"We'll send a taxicab for you."

They do send taxicabs for you and then they dump you out at the theatre, and it's a case of each man for himself and get the women and children first. There's al-

most always an amateur stage manager, and he knows practically nothing about theatre, except what he had read in William Archer, whom he knows well.

"We'll see that you go on as soon as you arrive," they tell you. This holds true if you get to the theatre before 9:30. In that case you not only go on but you stay on, for no other acts have arrived. You think you're through, but the stage manager signals and sometimes even bellows frantically that you're to please stay where you are.

After 9:30 you can do your act to the pleasing accompaniment of the bedlam raised in the wings by the boys and girls in their gentlemanly argument as to who goes on next. Frequently this is settled by a rush on stage, and it is just as well if you don't get in the way.

Another pleasing thing is to walk on after you've been introduced as "Lew Fields, known from coast to coast for his masterly support of Earle Williams in *Posita*." This is only slightly less pleasing than to see the billing for the benefit for the first time and to read, in large

With Baby LeRoy

type, that Miss Lottie Simpson, who, you later find, is the unmarried daughter of the lady chairman of the to-be-benefited society, will appear in person, assisted in agate type by Will Rogers, Raymond Hitchcock, Fannie Brice, George White, and others.

I know nothing that I would rather do than give my services for some worthy benefit. There has been much talk of an organization that, to repeat a phrase coined early in this piece, was going to separate the sheep from the goats. I'd like to get its address.

I know that very often the actor gives the organization that is staging the benefit at least as much trouble as he receives. For example, a few weeks ago, at a benefit at which I assisted in a private home, a young man arrived and handed the amateur manager of the affair a piece of cardboard as big as a door. On it, in large letters, was printed:

"Open—red and blue—also one-third dim whites. When fishermen exit bring whites full up. Second, when girl starts to sing dim to reds and blues again. Finish of her dance full white. Third, when girl exits red and blue

for man's song; finish white up. Fourth, girl sings, dim to red and blue. Finish up, kill reds and blues. Fifth, at music for last number dim to black-out. Stay out for bows. Note—reds and blues stay on."

"And what," said the amateur manager, a gentleman nevertheless, "might this be?"

"Just a light plot," said the actor.

"Oh," said the amateur manager, who was a bit of a wit, as I later learned, "if you ever went in for a complete scenario, what a wordy bird you'd be."

But there aren't many moments like this. Mostly, it's hanging around in the wings—for, of course, no one knows where your dressing room is—hoping that all of the audience won't go home, because they have a hard working day ahead of them tomorrow and they only came in the first place to oblige Aunt Ella, who was forced to buy the tickets from that Moore person, before you go on.

To repeat an act or two of *Poppy* is the least of the requests I get.

At smaller gatherings, in ballrooms and such, there is a determined and active minority that insists upon trying on your trick mustache.

There is also a persistent group of managers in such places who think juggling is at its best in dark corners or, preferably, without lights.

I repeat, no one is more willing than I am to do everything in the world for legitimate benefits. (In this connection I am even minded to say a few words about the difference between the sheep and the goats.) But it is high time, I think, that benefits were given and not thrown.

November 25, 1923

ANYTHING FOR A LAUGH

by W.C.Fields

I have spent years working out gags to make people laugh. With the patience of an old mariner making a ship in a bottle, I have been able to build situations that have turned out to be funny. But—to show you what a crazy way this is to make a living—the biggest laugh on the stage I ever got was an almost exact reproduction of an occurrence one evening when I was visiting a friend, and it took no thinking-up whatsoever.

At my friend's home it didn't even get a snicker, but in the theater it caused the audience to yell for a full minute.

On the stage I was a pompous nobody. The telephone rang. I told my wife I would answer it, in a manner that showed I doubted she was capable of handling an affair of such importance.

I said, "Hello, Elmer. . . . Yes, Elmer. . . . Is that so, Elmer? . . . Of course, Elmer. . . . Good-by, Elmer."

I hung up the receiver and said to my wife, as though I were disclosing a state secret, "That was Elmer."

It was a roar. It took ten or twelve performances to find that "Elmer" is the funniest name for a man. I tried them all—Charley, Clarence, Oscar, Archibald, Luke, and dozens of others—but Elmer was tops. That was several years ago. Elmer is still funny—unless your name happens to be Elmer. In that case you probably will vote for Clarence.

I don't know why the scene turned out to be so terribly funny. The funniest thing about comedy is that you never know why people laugh. I know *what* makes them laugh, but trying to get your hands on the *why* of it is like trying to pick an eel out of a tub of water.

"Charley Bogle," spoken slowly and solemnly with a very long "o," is a laugh. "George Beebe" is not funny, but "Doctor Beebe" is. The expression "You big Swede"

Signing autographs for servicemen during the filming of Follow the Boys

is not good for a laugh, but "You big Polack" goes big. But if you say "You big Polack" in a show you'll be visited by indignant delegations of protesting Poles. The Swedes don't seem to mind.

Usually towns that have a "ville" on the end of the name—like Jonesville—are not to be taken seriously, while those that begin with "Saint" cannot be joked about. But will you tell me why St. Louis goes well in a gag and Louisville does not?

It's difficult to put over a joke about any of the Southern states. They go best in sentimental songs. Northern states are different. A fellow from New Jersey, Iowa, Kansas, or Minnesota can be funny (except to natives of

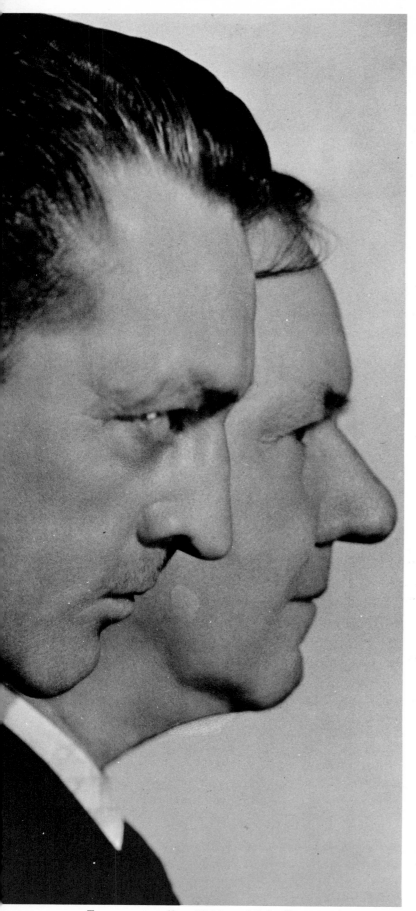

Two great profiles: Fields and John Barrymore

those states) but if his birthplace, in the plot, is Virginia or Tennessee he has to be a straight man.

I don't know the why of all this—any more than I know why a man gets sore if he slips and falls, while if a woman falls, she laughs. Nor why it is harder to put over comedy in Kansas City than in any other city in the United States, and easier in New York.

Flo Ziegfeld never thought a comedy act was any good unless there was a beautiful girl in it, and he picked on me when I was doing my golf game in the *Follies*.

It was a scene in which I came on the golf course with a caddy and had trouble for eighteen minutes without ever hitting the ball. Lionel Barrymore told me it was the funniest gag he ever saw—and you can't laugh off a testimonial like that!

One day Ziegfeld saw a picture in a paper showing a society girl with a Russian wolfhound. He dropped the paper, ran out, bought a wolfhound, and told me he was going to have Dolores, one of his glorified girls, walk across the stage leading the hound, in the middle of my act!

I squawked, but it didn't do any good, and at the next performance, just as I was building up laughs by stepping in a pie that somebody had left on the golf course, out of the wings—for no reason except that Ziegfeld had told her to do it—comes Dolores, with slow, stately tread, leading the Russian wolfhound.

I lost my audience instantly. They didn't know what it was all about. I wasn't going to give up my scene without a fight, so I looked at Dolores in amazement, and then at the audience as if I, too, were shocked at this strange sight on the golf course. When she was halfway across the stage I said, "That's a very beautiful horse."

It got a big laugh.

Dolores was so indignant because I had spoiled her parade, that she grabbed the hound around the shoulders and ran off the stage with him in her arms—and that was another laugh.

Ziegfeld and Dolores raised the very devil. I maintained that I had improved the scene. They said I had ruined it, and finally we compromised. I was to let her have her moment and was not to speak the line until she was one step from her exit. It turned out that the suspence made it all the better.

I experimented night after night to find out what animal was the funniest. I finally settled upon "That's a very beautiful camel."

Usually there is nothing funny about horses—except prop horses with two men inside—but one of Ed Wynn's best gags was where he sat down in a restaurant and said, "I'm so hungry I could eat a horse," and the waiter went out and led in a live horse.

You usually can't get a laugh out of damaging anything valuable. When you kick a silk hat, it must be dilapidated; when you wreck a car, bang it up a little before you bring it on the scene.

Herbert Marshall and Gloria Swanson visit the set of Poppy

Yet Harold Lloyd had a great gag when he drove out proudly in a new, expensive car which immediately was commandeered by police, chasing bandits. The car was shot full of holes, and then it stalled on a railroad track. Lloyd jumped out and tried to start it, a train came along and hit it, and all he had left was the starting crank which he held in his hand.

It is funnier to bend things than to break them—bend the fenders on a car in a comedy wreck, don't tear them off. In my golf game, which I have been doing for years, at first I swung at the ball and broke the club. Now I bend it at a right angle. If one comedian hits another over the head with a crowbar, the crowbar should bend, not break. In legitimate drama, the hero breaks his sword, and it is dramatic. In comedy, the sword bends, and stays bent.

There is something funny about mice and for years, without success, I tried to get a good gag about them. An accident finally gave it to me.

In *Poppy*, I was a small-time confidence man whose philosophy, you may remember, was "Never give a sucker an even break." In one scene I was alone in a dark library, hunting on tiptoe for cards that I intended to mark, so that later I could cheat in a poker game. One night, as I was stealing around the stage, being careful not to wake up anybody in the house, somebody, off-stage, accidentally knocked over a pile of boxes with a crash that shook the theater.

My scene was ruined for the moment. I had an inspiration. I stole down to the footlights and whispered across to the audience, "Mice!"

We kept that in the act, too.

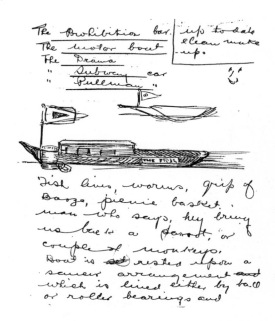

Professors of Humor will tell you the audience must not be allowed to guess what is coming, that humor is always based upon surprise. The theory is often true, but in *You're Telling Me*, my most recent moving picture, I have a scene in which the laugh depends upon the fact that the audience knows in advance exactly what is going to happen.

I play a stupid and self-important inventor and I explain the details of my new burglar trap. According to my plan, I shall become friendly with the burglar, invite him to sit down and talk things over, and, when he sits

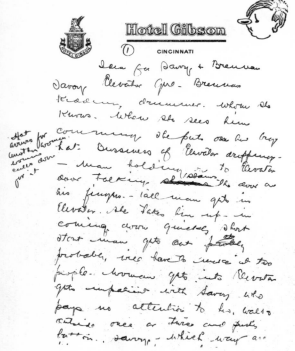

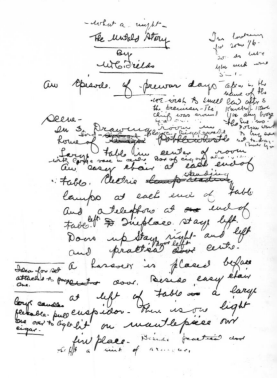

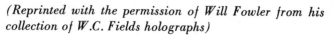

Jottings by the great man, including a self-caricature   *(Reprinted with the permission of Will Fowler from his collection of W.C. Fields holographs)*

in a chair, a lever will automatically release an immense iron ball which will hit him, *Socko!*, on the head and kill him instantly.

From that moment the audience knows what's coming —that pretty soon I'll forget about the iron ball and will sit in the chair myself. The laughter begins when I start toward the chair. It reaches its peak *before* the ball whams me on the bean.

If I sat in a chair and the ball fell on my head, and *then* it was explained that it was a burglar alarm, the scene would fall flat.

The success of the scene depends upon the absence of surprise.

I know we laugh at the troubles of others, provided those troubles are not too serious. Out of that observation I have reached a conclusion which may be of some comfort to those accused of "having no sense of humor." These folks are charming, lovable, philanthropic people, and invariably I like them—as long as they keep out of the theaters where I am playing, which they usually do. If they get in by mistake, they leave early.

The reason they don't laugh at most gags is that their first emotional reaction is to feel sorry for people instead of to laugh at them.

I like, in an audience, the fellow who roars continuously at the troubles of the character I am portraying on the stage, but he probably has a mean streak in him and, if I needed ten dollars, he'd be the last person I'd call upon. I'd go first to the old lady and old gentleman back in Row S who keep wondering what there is to laugh at.

September, 1934

THE
FILMS

POOL
SHARKS

1915

CREDITS:

Produced and distributed by Gaumont Company. (Although a British company, the film was made in New York.) Running time: 1 reel.

SYNOPSIS:

This is the first film that W.C. Fields made and it stars him in his famous pool game, which he had performed many times before on the stage.

JANICE MEREDITH

1924

CREDITS:

Distributed by Metro-Goldwyn. Produced by Cosmopolitan Pictures. Directed by E. Mason Hopper. From the novel by Paul Leicester Ford. Screenplay by Lilly Hayward. Settings by Josef Crban. Musical score by Deems Taylor. Running time: 153 minutes.

CAST:

Janice Meredith	Marion Davies
Charles Fownes	Harrison Ford
Squire Meredith	Macklyn Arbuckle
General Washington	Joseph Kilgour
Lord Howe	George Nash
Lord Cornwallis	Tyrone Power
Susie	May Vokes
A British Sergeant	W.C. Fields
Philemon	Olin Howland
Mrs. Meredith	Hattie Delaro
Squire Hennion	Spencer Charters
Captain Mowbray	Douglas Stevenson
Mrs. Loring	Helen Lee Worthing

SYNOPSIS:

The story begins near Brunswick, N.J., in 1774 as a view is presented of the Tory household of the Merediths whose tea drinking and other pro-British attitudes and habits are being protested against by the Sons of Liberty. Janice, the heroine, is a vivacious young maid and a natural coquette, around whom many thrilling and famous episodes of the American revolution revolve. She subdues British hearts at Philadelphia, is a delight for the captives in Virginia, and conquers both friend and foe in the trenches of Yorktown. The story of her varying fortunes is capitally told, and one follows Janice and her fiery lover, Charles Fownes, through manifold wild adventures and hairbreadth escapes. Fownes fulfills perilous missions for the patriotic cause, undergoes the most trying ordeals and narrowly escapes being hanged as a spy. He exerts himself to the utmost to rescue the Meredith family from impending misfortunes and is misrepresented and unjustly accused of cruelty toward them. He becomes the trusted friend of General Washington, and in the end wins the hand and heart of the impulsive and capricious Janice. With the blessing of General and Mrs. Washington, Charles and Janice are happily united in marriage.

With Marion Davies   HARVEY STEWART

REVIEWS:

Weekly Variety

On its merits *Janice Meredith* is a whale of a program picture because of its scenic magnificence, but its scenario incongruities and inferior handling of some historic episodes keep it out of the $2.00 ticket class.

Motion Picture News

. . . with W.C. Fields playing some rich comedy as a drunken British sergeant.

SALLY OF THE SAWDUST

1925

CREDITS:

Distributed by United Artists. Produced by Paramount. Directed by D.W. Griffith. Adapted by Forrest Halsey from the stage play *Poppy* by Dorothy Donnelly. Photographed by Harry Fischbeck and Hal Sintzenich. Running time: 104 minutes.

CAST:

Sally	Carol Dempster
Professor Eustace McGargle	W.C. Fields
Peyton Lennox	Alfred Lunt
Judge Henry L. Foster	Erville Alderson
Mrs. Foster	Effie Shannon
Lennox, Sr.	Charles Hammond
The Detective	Roy Applegate
Miss Vinton	Florence Fair
Society Leader	Marie Shotwell
Leon, the Acrobat	Glenn Anders

Carole Dempster

With Carole Dempster

SYNOPSIS:

Because she married a circus man, Judge Foster casts his only daughter out, and just before her death a few years later she leaves her little girl in the care of her friend McGargle, a good-natured crook, juggler and faker. Sally, the girl, grows up in this atmosphere, unaware of her ancestry. McGargle, realizing his responsibility, finally manages to get a job with a carnival company playing at Great Meadows where the Fosters live. A real-estate boom has made them wealthy. Sally is a hit with her dancing and Peyton, the son of Judge Foster's friend, falls in love with her. To save him, the Judge arranges to have McGargle and Sally arrested. McGargle escapes but Sally is finally hunted down and brought back. McGargle, hearing of Sally's plight, swipes a flivver and, after many delays, reaches the courtroom and presents proof of Sally's parentage. The Judge dismisses the case and his wife takes Sally in her arms, but Peyton's claim is stronger and she agrees to become his wife. McGargle is persuaded to remain and found an outlet for his peculiar talents in selling real estate.

With Alfred Lunt

REVIEWS:

Weekly Variety

A cinch for the picture houses through its comedy, supplied mostly by W.C. Fields, with Carol Dempster's performance as Sally a delight. D.W. Griffith is down to common picture making in this one.

Moving Picture World

Mr. Fields is literally a wow and is guaranteed to go over big with any audience. He figures largely in this picture, and with a technique entirely different from the usual screen comedian gets a laugh or a chuckle almost the entire time he is on the screen. Obviously, Mr. Griffith had his eye on the box-office and did not hesitate to make certain sacrifices to get the effects he wanted.

With Carole Dempster

THAT ROYLE GIRL

1926

CREDITS:

Distributed by Paramount. Produced by Famous Players–Lasky Corporation. Produced and directed by D.W. Griffith. From the story by Edwin Balmer. Screenplay by Paul Scholfield. Photographed by Harry Fischbeck and Hal Sintzenich. Running time: 114 minutes.

CAST:

Joan Daisy Royle	Carol Dempster
Her Father	W.C. Fields
Calvin Clarke	James Kirkwood
Fred Ketlar	Harrison Ford
George Baretta	Paul Everton
Adele Ketlar	Kathleen Chambers
His Henchman	George Rigas
Baretta's "Girl"	Florence Auer
Mrs. Clarke	Ida Waterman
Clarke's Fiancée	Alice Laidley
Lola Nelson	Dorothea Love
Elman	Dore Davidson
Oliver	Frank Allworth
Hofer	Bobby Watson

SYNOPSIS:

Daisy Royle is the daughter of a crook. She meets Fred Ketlar, a jazz orchestra conductor, and falls in love with him. Ketlar's love for her is more or less physical. Ketlar's wife is killed, actually by a gangster, but Ketlar is accused. In this way Daisy is implicated and meets Calvin Clarke, the district attorney. He falls in love with her, but struggles against showing it, and she finds in him the qualities she has always wanted. So it works to the point where Daisy must prove to him that she is strictly on the level. With the help of a *Chicago Tribune* reporter, Daisy disguises herself and sets out to trap the gangster who killed Mrs. Ketlar. She gets into a private party at a roadhouse and hears enough to get Ketlar released. As she is phoning a woman grabs her, thereby causing a ruckus, which makes Clarke think she is in danger. She *is* in trouble, but after she eludes everyone, a terrible cyclone comes up and destroys the adjacent buildings. Even after the gangsters find her and cast her into a cellar, the storm continues with such fury that a flock of rafters fall on them and dispose of their villainy forever. Then come the district attorney and the clinch finish.

REVIEW:
Weekly Variety

In a vain effort to make a comedy, Griffith has dragged in W.C. Fields as the girl's father, but he doesn't belong in the picture, no matter how you look at it. Fields has nothing to do, and does it just like a man with nothing to do would do it. Although a long film with good melodrama and a marvelous cyclone scene, this film is the poorest thing Griffith has turned out in a great many years.

IT'S
THE OLD
ARMY GAME

1926

CREDITS:

Distributed by Famous Players—Lasky Corporation. Produced by Adolph Zukor and Jessie L. Lasky. Directed by Edward Sutherland. From the play by J.P. McEvoy. Screenplay by Thomas J. Geraghty. Photographed by Alvin Wychoff. Running time: 70 minutes.

CAST:

Elmer Prettywillie	W.C. Fields
Mildred Marshall	Louise Brooks
Tessie Overholt	Blanche Ring
George Parker	William Gaxton
Sarah Pancoast	Mary Foy
Mickey	Mickey Bennett

HARVEY STEWART

SYNOPSIS:

The story opens with a bedroom scene; Fields, as the village druggist, is asleep. An automobile containing a woman is seen coming down the road. The auto and a train just escape a collision and the woman is disclosed ringing the druggist's night bell. He awakes and opens the store. All she wants is a two-cent stamp. After the sale, the druggist tries to sleep, but the garbage collectors and others make sleep impossible. In mailing her letter, the woman rings the fire alarm, which brings the fire department swarming into the drugstore. But when they can't find a fire, they all sit down to have ice cream sodas. When the firemen leave, a fire begins, but the druggist is able to put it out with a cigar box while at the same time lighting a cigar for himself. Later in the day, he takes his family on a picnic to look over some real estate being sold in a new real-estate boom. The picnic ends with the wrecking of a Florida estate which he believes is up for sale.

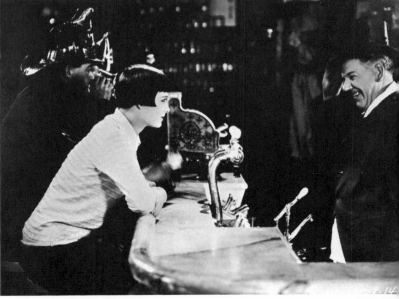

With Louise Brooks   HARVEY STEWART

HARVEY STEWART

REVIEWS:

Daily Variety

Succession of snappy gags make for a first-class laugh-provoker. W.C. Fields is first-rate as the hero, and Mickey Bennett is great as the kid.

Mordaunt Hall in *The New York Times*

It's The Old Army Game, the pictorial attraction featuring W.C. Fields, may not be a masterpiece of fun, but at any rate it is a subject that will create plenty of amusement. Mr. Fields is busy throughout this production largely in episodes borrowed from his stage skits. Mr. Fields' clever and energetic performance is helped along by the attractive Louise Brooks.

SO'S YOUR OLD MAN

1926

With Marcia Harris

CREDITS:

Produced and distributed by Famous Players–Lasky Corporation. Directed by Gregory La Cava. Adapted by Howard Emmett Rogers from *Mr. Bisbee's Princess* by Julian Street. Screenplay by J. Clarkson Miller. Running time: 67 minutes.

CAST:

Samuel Bisbee	W.C. Fields
Princess Lescaboura	Alice Joyce
Kenneth Murchison	Charles Rogers
Alice Bisbee	Kittins Reichert
Mrs. Bisbee	Marcia Harris
Mrs. Murchison	Julia Ralph
Jeff	Frank Montgomery
Al	Jerry Sinclair

SYNOPSIS:

Samuel Bisbee is a glazier in a small New Jersey town. He lives in a tumbled-down sort of a house with his wife and daughter, the latter a pretty girl courted by the son of the wealthy Murchisons. Young Murchison calls to inform the girl that his mother is going to visit that afternoon.

Mother arrives and all goes well until Pa Bisbee comes in from the shop in the back of the house, where he has been celebrating with a couple of old cronies.

He gums up the works but tells the haughty Mrs. Murchison that in a couple of days he is going to be as much

of the social elite as she is. He has invented an unbreak-
able glass for automobiles and has been asked to demon-
strate it before a convention of automobile men in Washington. He goes there, having his flivver equipped with
the glass, and parks it in front of the hotel while he goes
in to see the committee. Someone moves his car while he
is in the hotel. When he returns, armed with bricks and
a hammer, to go through with the test he picks another
flivver and smashes the glass. Then he selects another
with the same result and, to escape arrest, must beat it
without getting his own car.

Returning home on the train, he decides to end it all
with poison, but his bottle is smashed. A few minutes
later, when the train gives a lurch, he is thrown into the
stateroom of the Spanish princess. Noting a bottle of
iodine on the table before her, he believes she is ready
to take the same way out and starts to dissuade her.

As he relates his story, her sympathy is aroused and
she resolves to help the disappointed man out. She does
not tell him who she is, but says he may call her "Marie."

On the train with him are a couple of the village's old
women gossips. They spread the story of his ride with a
woman in a stateroom, and it is around the home town
like wildfire before he is back five minutes. To get up
courage to go home, he seeks out his serious drinking

pals and the trio stage a blast that lasts three days. Meantime the princess has announced her intention of visiting the little town, and the social elite arrange a reception but are flabbergasted when she asks for "Old Sam." The party starts for his home and runs across the old boy headed that way himself, having purchased a pony to present to the wife as a peace offering.

Society then accepts the Bisbees, for the princess remains at their home, and Sam is selected to tee off the first ball at the opening of a new country club. Then the chairman of the automen's convention arrives; having discovered the real car and tested the glass for himself, he found it was as claimed and is ready to hand over a million-dollar contract.

REVIEW:
Mordaunt Hall in *The New York Times*

This broad comedy was directed by Gregory LaCava, whose work, even in this picture, makes it apparent that his ability ought to be employed on more comprehensive stories. Once or twice Mr. Fields stoops a little low for his comedy, and, judging by its effect upon the spectators, it was not worth the risk. He has a number of ludicrous ideas, which at least betokens a lively imagination, despite the fact that they are hardly part and parcel of the prize story.

With Julia Ralph and Marcia Harris UNIVERSITY OF TEXAS

THE POTTERS

1927

CREDITS:

Distributed by Paramount. Produced by Famous Players—Lasky Corporation. Directed by Fred Newmeyer. Adapted by Sam Mintz and Ray Harris from J.P. McEvoy's play of the same name. Screenplay by J. Clarkson Miller. Photographed by P.C. Vogel. Running time: 71 minutes.

With Charles "Buddy" Rogers

CAST:

Pa Potter	W.C. Fields
Ma Potter	Mary Alden
Mamie	Ivy Harris
Bill	Jack Egan
Red Miller	"Skeets" Gallagher
Rankin	Joseph Smiley
Eagle	Bradley Barker

SYNOPSIS:

The Potters go through the usual squabbles, pleasures and disappointments of a typical average family. Pa Potter is the central figure in the difficulties that arise when he gullibly invests four thousand dollars of the family savings in some worthless oil stock without Ma's consent. However, when the family's problems reach a low ebb, new oil is found in the old wells and they become rich.

REVIEWS:

Mordaunt Hall in *The New York Times*

Only too rarely does a comedy as good as *The Potters* come to Broadway, and it is not very often that a comedian gives as clever a performance as W.C. Fields does in the screen version of J.P. McEvoy's play. Another distinct point about this brilliant piece of work is that the director, Fred Newmeyer, co-operating with the adaptors of the stage effort, has not permitted the romance between the two young people to block the trend of the

With Mary Alden   HARVEY STEWART

With Richard (Skeets) Gallagher, Ivy Harris, and Mary Alden

chronicle, which usually happens in motion pictures. Hence *The Potters* is an exceptionally satisfactory entertainment.

Mr. Fields' portrayal of "Pa" Potter is a joy, a characterization which reveals that this stage veteran has studied his previous film work and checked his extravagant tendencies. So well suited to this part is Mr. Fields that one wonders whether anyone could ever have rivaled his performance. Throughout the incidents Mr. Fields delivers natural and fine reflections of "Pa" Potter's changeable moods. He goes from satisfaction to disappointment, to irritability and then to a display of uncontrollable joy. In the stretch wherein he throws everything around the room and does handsprings one is reminded of Chaplin's antics in a scene in *The Gold Rush*.

With Mary Alden   HARVEY STEWART

RUNNING WILD

1927

CREDITS:

Produced and distributed by Paramount. Written and directed by Gregory La Cava. Adaptation and screenplay by Roy Briant. Photographed by Paul Vogel. Running time: 68 minutes.

CAST:

Elmer Finch	W.C. Fields
Elizabeth	Mary Brian
Jerry Harvey	Claud Buchanan
Mrs. Finch	Marie Shotwell
Junior	Barney Raskle
Mr. Harvey	Frederick Burton
Mr. Johnson	J. Moy Bennett
Amos Barker	Frank Evans
Arvo, the Hypnotist	Ed Roseman
Truckdriver	Tom Madden
Rex	Himself

With Mary Brian and Marie Shotwell

HARVEY STEWART

SYNOPSIS:

Elmer Finch suffers from an unusually pronounced case of an inferiority complex. His second wife browbeats him and it would be overpolite to say his own daughter is a problem. His stepson, a fat specimen, makes fun of Elmer and sets the dog after him. A stentorian tone causes Finch to quiver. But he becomes an altogether different individual when he is hypnotized by a stage magician. The spell is not broken and he returns home still believing himself a lion. His manner and attitude surprise all. Finch's outbursts startle his wife, cow her son, and give him a position of power for the first time. His courage permits him to make a contract for which the commission is fifteen thousand dollars. When the spell is broken, Elmer realizes the gains he has made. He feels courage, and everyone else is happy with the money Elmer has brought into the home.

With Mary Brian   HARVEY STEWART

With Marie Shotwell   HARVEY STEWART

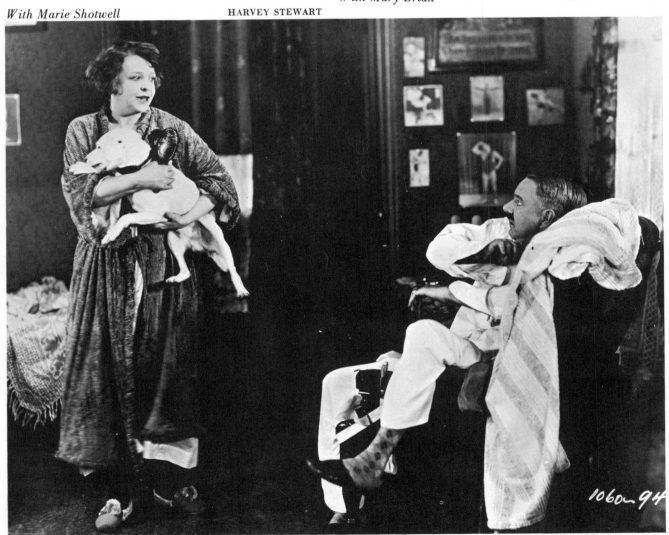

With Marie Shotwell and Mary Brian   HARVEY STEWART

REVIEWS:

Motion Picture News

It has taken W.C. Fields several pictures to get going. His *Running Wild* enters the gallery, well fortified with chuckles—many of which come deep from the diaphragm. The comedian has discarded his "Follies Tricks"—tricks, you might say, which were keeping him back. In this offering he demonstrates he has some different aces up his sleeve.

Mordaunt Hall in *The New York Times*

There are times when this comedy is really good, but quite often Mr. Fields overdoes the fun, with the result that it falls somewhat flat. He was, as a matter of fact, far more comic in the screen version of *The Potters*, which goes to prove that a sound adaptation of a well-knit stage comedy is better than the haphazard inspiration of those who are only concerned with the making of movies. There was a marked restraint about the picturization of *The Potters*, while in this current subject Mr. Fields manifests a fondness for returning to his extravagant actions, and plausibility is flung to the four winds.

TWO FLAMING YOUTHS

1927

CREDITS:

Produced and distributed by Paramount. Produced and directed by John Waters. Screenplay by Percy Heath and Donald Davis from an original story by Percy Heath. Titles by Jack Conway and Herman J. Manckewiecz. Running time: 55 minutes.

With Chester Conklin

CAST:

Gabby Gilfoil	W.C. Fields
Sheriff Ben Holden	Chester Conklin
Mary Gilfoil	Mary Brian
Tony Holden	Jack Luden
Simeon Trott	George Irving
Madge Malarkey	Cissy Fitzgerald
Slippery Sawtelle	Jimmie Quinn

SYNOPSIS:

Gabby Gilfoil is the financially embarrassed carnival showman, who, with his troupe of hungry freaks clamoring for food and wages, invades the county of which Ben Holden is sheriff. Holden is giving Madge Malarkey the heavy rush, with matrimony in view; but Gilfoil, a suave-mannered man, also clicks with the woman hotel owner. Gilfoil's intentions, however, are ulterior; he is counting on the woman's money to help pay his bills.

Complications follow: the sheriff mistakes the showman for a wanted criminal on whom there is a fifteen hundred dollar reward. Later, two rival county sheriffs claim the reward, with each wrestling for physical possession of the real Slippery Sawtelle.

Gabby Gilfoil is quick to capitalize on every opportunity for ticket sales. So when Sheriff Ben Holden is accidentally catapulted into a dugout containing a boxing kangaroo and cannot escape, but is forced to continue boxing with the trained animal, Gilfoil seizes the opportunity and vends tickets for the unusual event between the pugilistic animal and the unwilling sheriff. Gilfoil does well enough with his ticket sales to please his troupe. The finale has wealthy Simeon Trott marrying Madge,

With Mary Brian

leaving both the rivals for that fickle mama's heart, hand, and hotel good friends but without hope of having Madge or her pocketbook. To compensate for the loss of Madge, Sheriff Ben Holden plays a shell game with Madge's new husband, and wins a good sum, which he splits with Gilfoil.

REVIEW:
Mordaunt Hall in *The New York Times*

The background of these animated scenes is a circus, and the characters include a crook, an unlucky showman, a feather-brained sheriff and a green-eyed blonde. Mr. Fields acts the part of Gabby Gilfoil, the unfortunate circus man who attracts mud, rain, and almost anything except crowds. Toward the end of this somewhat dizzy affair Gilfoil proves himself to be quite Barnumesque. This happens when Sheriff Holden accidentally is catapulted into the section set aside for the boxing kangaraoo. Holden can't get away from the animal, and to protect himself he uses his fists. But so does the kangaroo, and therefore, Gilfoil makes a snappy spiel to the crowd, calling attention to the remarkable attraction of a sheriff fighting a kangaroo, and then proceeds to rake in the greenbacks. From that time on life takes a rosier hue for Gilfoil.

Catapults, mud, water, and other old reliables are brought into play in this film. The youngster who takes pot-shots at the Sheriff with a bean-shooter has some narrow escapes, particularly when he shatters a bottle of perfume the Sheriff happens to be taking over to Madge Malarkey, the bewitching but somewhat plump blonde. The odor of the bottle's contents causes the Sheriff to be eyed with suspicion by several characters, including Gilfoil, who himself is rather partial to Madge.

Sometimes John Waters, the director, ought to have been able to do more with the ability of these first water comedians. It is invariably a sign of weakness when water and mud have to be employed in an effort to tickle the risibles of the audience. Nonetheless it is a funny picture, obstreperous in many places, but quite diverting. Mr. Fields is a resourceful performer and his tricks are his own. He is also a good pantomimist, one who does not have to pretend that the rest of the world is deaf because he is acting for the "silent screen."

With Chester Conklin

TILLIE'S PUNCTURED ROMANCE

1928

CREDITS:

Distributed by Paramount. Produced by the Christie Studio. Directed by Edward Sutherland. Scenario by Monte Brice and Keene Thompson based on characters from an earlier film of the same title. Photographed by William Wheeler and Charles Boyle. Edited by A. Huffsmith. Running time: 57 minutes.

CAST:

The Ring Master	W.C. Fields
Tillie, a runaway girl	Louise Fazenda
The Circus Owner	Chester Conklin
Tillie's Father	Mack Swain
The Heroine	Doris Hill
The Hero	Grant Withers
The Property Man	Tom Kennedy
The Strong Woman	Babe London
The Midget	Billy Platt

and Kalla Pasha, Mickey Bennett, Mike Rafetto, and Baron von Dobeneck

With Tom Kennedy

Louise Fazenda

Chester Conklin

SYNOPSIS:

A farm girl runs off and joins the circus, which is run by Conklin and has Fields as the ringmaster who is plotting to get his boss into the lion's cage to finish him off, so he (Fields) can take over the circus. Then when World War I breaks out, the circus goes overseas to entertain the army. The circus helps the Allied cause to a great extent by joining the German army and causing great confusion.

Chester Conklin and Louise Fazenda

With Chester Conklin and Louise Fazenda

With Chester Conklin

FOOLS FOR LUCK

1928

CREDITS:

Produced and distributed by Paramount. Directed by Charles F. Reisner. Screenplay by J. Walter Ruben. Title writer: George Marion. Photographed by William Marshall. Editor: George Nichols, Jr. Running time: 60 minutes.

CAST:

Richard Whitehead	W.C. Fields
Samuel Hunter	Chester Conklin
Louise Hunter	Sally Blane
Ray Caldwell	Jack Luden
Mrs. Hunter	Mary Alden
Charles Grogan	Arthur Housman
Jim Simpson	Robert Dudley
Mrs. Simpson	Martha Mattox

With Chester Conklin and others

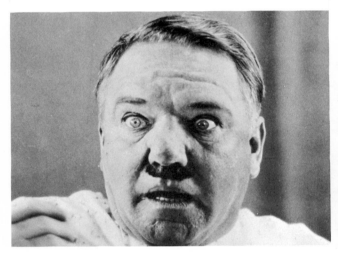

SYNOPSIS:

Mr. Whitehead, a scheming man, approaches Sam Hunter, the richest man in Huntersville, to invest in oil. However, when the deal is concluded, it is discovered that there is no longer any oil in these wells. Various fights and arguments over the matter interrupt Sam's daughter's romance, besides annoying Mr. Hunter. However, oil is rediscovered in the supposedly dry wells; when the money begins to roll in, all problems are solved to everyone's delight.

With Sally Blane and Chester Conklin

REVIEWS:

Mordaunt Hall in *The New York Times*

Both Mr. Conklin and Mr. Fields are far better in more intelligent stories than this current specimen. They are either very funny in their films or very silly. In this one the silly ideas predominate.

Motion Picture Herald

The comedy-team pictures are fast losing their sting. Let a couple of comedians repeat their oft-tried gags too often and nothing much of consequence is left to make a fuss over. W.C. Fields and Chester Conklin try hard to make this one mirthful, but it grows tiresome long before the finish is reached. Each funmaker uses the other as a foil, but the stuff just isn't there.

THE GOLF SPECIALIST

1930

CREDITS:

A Radio Pictures Presentation, distributed by R.K.O. Produced by Louis Brock. Directed by Monte Brice. Running time: 20 minutes.

SYNOPSIS:

The film is a two-reeler presenting Fields in the famous golf act he had often used on the stage prior to this film. This was his first sound film.

HER MAJESTY LOVE

1931

With Marilyn Miller

CREDITS:

Produced and distributed by Warners. Directed by William Dieterle. Screenplay by Robert Lord and Arthur Caesar from original story by R. Berbrauer and R. Oesterreicher. Dialogue by Henry Blanke and Joseph Jackson. Editor: Ralph Dawson. Art direction by Jack Okey. Photographed by Robert Kurrle. Lyrics by Al Dubin. Running time: 75 minutes.

CAST:

Lia Toerrek	Marilyn Miller
Fred von Wellingen	Ben Lyon
Lia's Father	W.C. Fields
Otmar	Ford Sterling
Baron von Schwarzdorf	Leon Errol
Emil	Chester Conklin
Hanneman	Harry Stubbs
Aunt Harriette	Maude Eburne
Reisenfeld	Harry Holman
Factory Secretary	Ruth Hall
The "Third" Man	William Irving
Fred's Sister, Elli	Mae Madison

and Clarence Wilson and Virginia Sale

65

Ben Lyon and Marilyn Miller

With Marilyn Miller and Leon Errol

SYNOPSIS:

Lia Toerrek, an ordinary girl, has fallen in love with Fred von Wellingen, son of a wealthy family. But Lia's uncouth father has spent most of his life as a juggler with a traveling show. He therefore has the irresistible desire to do a little juggling with chocolate eclairs and so forth. This is all very well when he is alone at a table, but later when he joins Fred's relatives at a formal dinner—after Fred has announced his engagement to Lia—and tosses pastries from one end of the table to a plate held by a man at the other end, the snobbish von Wellingens are aghast. His announcement that he is a barber and that Lia is a barmaid further shocks the assembly, who then observe the proud father juggling three plates, which all fall to the floor when Lia remonstrates with him for having imbibed too many brandies.

It is no wonder that the von Wellingen family is anxious to have Fred break the engagement. The young man signs a contract whereby he is made general manager of the family industry at a salary of ten thousand marks a month, so long as he agrees not to marry Lia. Since the engagement is off, Baron von Schwarzdorf, a bachelor playboy never without a monocle, offers his title to Lia. Fred is miserable and so is Lia, but she nonetheless consents to marry the Baron. The marriage is arranged and takes place in Berlin. At the last minute Fred decides to fly to Berlin and stop the marriage. He arrives too late, however, just as the ceremony ends. But Lia and Fred are so overjoyed to see each other that they walk off happily together, leaving the Baron and the wedding guests behind.

REVIEW:
The New York Times

There are dozens of clever touches, so good that one cannot but hope that some day Mr. Dieterle will be rewarded by a narrative more worthy of his artistry and fertile brain. Mr. W.C. Fields aroused a good deal of laughter as did Mr. Errol and Mr. Sterling.

With Marilyn Miller and Leon Errol

MILLION DOLLAR LEGS

1932

CREDITS:

Produced and distributed by Paramount. Directed by Edward Cline. Screenplay by Henry Myers and Nick Barrows from a story by Joseph L. Mankiewicz. Photographed by Arthur Todd. Running time: 64 minutes.

CAST:

Migg Tweeny	Jack Oakie
The President	W.C. Fields
The Major-Domo	Andy Clyde
Mata Machree	Lyda Roberti
Angela	Susan Fleming
Mysterious Man	Ben Turpin
Secretary of the Treasury	Hugh Herbert
Mr. Baldwin	George Barbier
Willie (Angela's Brother)	Dickie Moore
Secretary of the Interior	Billy Gilbert
Secretary of Agriculture	Vernon Dent
Secretary of War	Teddy Hart
Secretary of Labor	John Sinclair
Secretary of State	Sam Adams
Secretary of the Navy	Irving Bacon
Ship's Captain	Ben Taggart
Customs Inspector	Hank Mann
Jumper	Chick Collins
Starter at the Games	Sid Saylor

SYNOPSIS:

In the mythological country of Klopstokia, where everyone is a sports addict and babies can jump six feet and practically every adult can run the mile in a few seconds, problems continually arise. It is decided by the government officials that they will enter the Olympic Games, to be played this time in the United States. But constant intrigue in government circles, a mysterious man, and national problems endanger their success, in spite of their having the best of all possible athletes.

REVIEWS:

Alexander Bakshy in *The Nation*

Joseph L. Mankiewicz, the author of the story providing the basis for *Million Dollar Legs*, and his adapters have clearly fallen far short of producing a masterpiece. But they did let their fancy run as far as it would carry them, and the result is a film that at times has a quality of freshness and genuine imagination much too rare in Hollywood products. The best moments in the film are the episodes describing the crazy system of government which rules in the Republic of Klopstokia. What with the arm-pulling contests, which is the Klopstokian way of electing a president, and the constant popping up of mysterious spies, who include the inimitable Ben Turpin, cross-eyed, be-cloaked, and with a notebook in his hand, the story starts off in the true mood of reckless extravaganza. Unfortunately, this mood does not last.

While being thankful for small mercies, one cannot help regretting that the film fails to rise to its opportunities in two other respects aside from its tame ending. Here was a story that seemed to cry for a fantastic treatment on the lines of René Clair's *Le Million*. Yet all we get in the film is a routine linking of scenes with not the slightest attempt to give them a crazy and sweeping rhythm that would reflect the mood of its story.

The other missed opportunity one can hardly hope to see realized in Hollywood. There is implicit satire in the Klopstokian methods of government. But to bring it out and stress its points would have required courage and independence of mind, and when has Hollywood shown that it had any of these qualities or cared for them?

With Susan Fleming

With Susan Fleming

With Jack Oakie

Motion Picture Herald

Don't let the critical reviews on this picture affect you too much. Some of them are not likely to be very complimentary. But from a showman's point of view, Paramount has tried an experiment with *Million Dollar Legs* that may set a new note in the production of talking pictures.

Here's what they've done: they have gone back to the dark ages of motion picture production and adapted in this picture all those great laugh-creating ideas that made motion pictures the fourth greatest industry in the country. Slapstick, belly-laughs, damnfool nonsense, chases; they're all there, plus a load of gags that can't fail to provoke howls of laughter. They make a monkey of the hero and Jack Oakie does one sweet job in a part that

many another star would be afraid to tackle for fear of injuring his reputation. In short, Paramount lifted a whole book-full of pages from the "Triangle-Keystone Cop" days, when nobody knew what a script was—when they made the picture as they went along and where everyone's craziest ideas were incorporated in the film, if it looked as though they had any possible chance of bringing a laugh.

Never for one minute is it serious. In fact its absurdity is really so fine that we warned you in the beginning not to pay too much attention to critics, who, in their enthusiasm to review the picture in line with the present-day trend, may miss the real point of the whole nonsensical farce.

IF
I HAD
A MILLION

1932

With Alison Skipworth

With Alison Skipworth

CAST:

Gallagher	Gary Cooper
Violet	Wynne Gibson
Eddie Jackson	George Raft
The Clerk	Charles Laughton
John Glidden	Richard Bennett
Mulligan	Jack Oakie
Mary Wallace	Frances Dee
Henry Peabody	Charlie Ruggles
Emily	Allison Skipworth
Rollo	W.C. Fields
Mrs. Peabody	Mary Boland
O'Brien	Roscoe Karns
Mrs. Walker	May Robson
John Wallace	Gene Raymond
Zeb	Lucien Littlefield
Marie	Joyce Compton

CREDITS:

Produced and distributed by Paramount. Directed by Ernst Lubitsch, Norman Taurog, Stephen Roberts, Norman McLeod, James Cruze, William A. Seiter, and H. Bruce Humberstone. Screenplay by Claude Binyon, Whitney Bolton, Malcolm Stuart Boylan, John Bright, Sidney Buchman, Lester Cole, Isabel Dawn, Boyce DeGaw, Walter DeLeon, Oliver H. P. Garrett, Harvey Gates, Grover Jones, Ernst Lubitsch, Lawton Mackaill, Joseph L. Mankewicz, William Slavens McNutt, Seton I. Miller, and Tiffany Thayer from a story by Robert D. Andrews. Running time: 88 minutes.

With Alison Skipworth and Lucien Littlefield

SYNOPSIS:

John Glidden, a very wealthy man, prefers to give his fortune to strangers rather than have his relatives squabbling over it after he has gone. The story concerns his gift to several different people, who use the money for various purposes. First, we see Henry Peabody, a bedeviled clerk at home and at his work, wreck a china shop and proclaim his financial and domestic independence. Then Violet, a hardboiled sailor's sweetheart, uses the money she receives to move from the squalor of a back alley hideaway to the class of a Park Avenue apartment. But a million is the worst thing that could be handed to the clever crook, Eddie Jackson. He swaps his check for a "flop," and the "flophouse" keeper, who thinks that Eddie is crazy, burns up the check and yells for the cops.

Finally freed from his place of harsh employment, a downtrodden clerk ascends a long flight of stairs to give his boss a resounding raspberry. Three marines sell their million dollars for ten bucks because they think it's a phony, making Zeb, the buyer, rich. Rollo and Emily, a pair of oldtime ham actors, buy a fleet of secondhand cars and go about wrecking roadhogs. There is drama as John Wallace's check will not save him from the electric chair, even though it makes him financially independent. Mrs. Walker uses her windfall to turn a rigidly ruled Old Ladies' Home into a veritable heaven on earth for forgotten grandmothers.

REVIEWS:
Alexander Bakshy in *The Nation*

Were Hollywood as capable of grasping the moral of *If I Had A Million* as the public is likely to be, this production would mark an important advance toward a more intelligent conception of what constitutes an interesting film story. For the film is different from the usual run. Unfolding a series of independent episodes related to one another only through the general premise of what people are likely to do when they suddenly become rich, *If I Had A Million* proves conclusively that an interesting idea has as much power to cast a spell over the mind of the audience as any amount of complications in the dramatic plot. In the case of the film under review this power is demonstrated in spite of the mediocre quality of many of the individual stories which make up the narrative. If the film can only succeed in convincing Hollywood that intelligence adds value to its productions, it will have performed an important service in raising American films from the mire of cheap sentiment and hokum.

Motion Picture Herald

Maybe the basic idea of *If I Had A Million* is nothing new under the sun of motion picture production, but the startling technique adapted by Paramount in bringing this unusual work to the screen is ample evidence that there is something radically new under the Kleig lights in the way of imagination-capturing novelty.

Seven directors had a hand in directing the picture, yet it is almost impossible to determine just where and when each one entered. Eighteen writers prepared it for the screen, still it is one coherent story. Fourteen noted stars and a host of minor players appeared in it, but none of their appearances is dependent on those that precede or succeed them—save Richard Bennett as John Glidden. Contrary to the saying that too many cooks spoil the broth, it's a clever demonstration that the more brains and talent that work in a picture the better it is. Further, it does not even remotely resemble any of those experimental revues or parades of stars reminiscent of the musical comedy days. Rather it's a logical yarn based on one idea and having ten varying ramifications. It runs the range of entertainment from ribald, slapstick comedy to stark, tear-jerking melodrama.

With Alison Skipworth

FOUR MACK SENNETT SHORTS

(In 1932-1933 W.C. Fields made four short films for Mack Sennett.)

THE DENTIST

1932

CREDITS:

Distributed by Paramount. Produced by Mack Sennett. Directed by Leslie Pearce. Screenplay by W.C. Fields. Running time: 20 minutes.

CAST:

W.C. Fields and Babe Kane

REVIEW:

Motion Picture Herald

It is only after the very absent-minded W.C. Fields first indulges in a lot of smart gab with Babe Kane, then wrestles around with a cake of ice and plays a golf game strikingly reminiscent of his Ziegfeld "Follies" acts, that this grand comedy gets into his dentistry office. It reaches its best when Fields tends to the dental requirements of two feminine patients. A wrestling match tooth-extraction gag is provocative of laughs and a final adventure is with a heavily whiskered man, upon whom Fields uses a stethoscope to find his mouth and brings a shotgun into use when he flushes a covey of birds from the bushels of hair. Fine dialogue is delivered in the typical Fields fashion.

THE FATAL GLASS OF BEER

March 1933

CREDITS:

Distributed by Paramount. Produced by Mack Sennett. Directed by Clyde Bruckman. Original screenplay by W.C. Fields. Running time: 21 minutes.

CAST:

W.C. Fields, Rosemary Theby, George Chandler, and Rychard Cramer

SYNOPSIS:

W.C. Fields is a northwoods trapper, who tells a wild tale about his son being lured to a fall through drink.

REVIEWS:

Motion Picture Herald

Silly, but at the same time fairly amusing, is this comedy in which W.C. Fields, as the hunter in the northern woods, sings the song of the fatal glass of beer, and the boy who was lured by temptation in the big city. A flashback shows the boy, Field's son, in the city, being tempted. Home again from prison, the boy repents and a surprise finish has a bit of laughter. On the whole the comedy is hardly more than moderately entertaining.

Reactions from theater owners, as printed in the *Motion Picture Herald*, July 8, 1933:

J.E. Weber, Princess Theater, Chelsea Michigan—"Two reels of film and 20 minutes wasted."

J.J. Medford, Orpheum Theater, Oxford, N.C.—"This is the worst comedy we have played from any company this season. No story, no acting, and as a whole has nothing."

THE PHARMACIST

April 1933

CREDITS:

Distributed by Paramount. Produced by Mack Sennett. Directed by Arthur Ripley. Original story and screenplay by W.C. Fields. Running time: 20 minutes.

CAST:

W.C. Fields, Babe Kane, Elise Cavanna, Grady Sutton and Lorena Carr

SYNOPSIS:

A unified anthology of many of Mr. Fields' standard store gags. Fields as Dr. Dilweg, the pharmacist, runs a neighborhood shop. Business is good, he's been doing a land-office business selling postage stamps ever since he put up the neon sign. His wife and two daughters are the bane of his existence. The older daughter spends her time talking to her new boy friend Cuthbert on the telephone. The younger daughter refuses to eat her spinach but has developed a taste for the pet canary.

THE BARBER SHOP

July 1933

CREDITS:

Distributed by Paramount. Produced by Mack Sennett. Directed by Arthur Ripley. Original screenplay by W.C. Fields. Running time: 21 minutes.

CAST:

W.C. Fields, Elise Cavanna, Harry Watson, and Dagmar Oakland

SYNOPSIS:

O'Hair, a smalltown barber, has a field day trying to ply his trade while walking a tightrope between his beastly wife and his pretty manicurist. One of his customers, while getting a shave, inquires why a little dog is sitting beside the chair begging. "It's a funny thing about that dog," Fields muses, "one day I was shaving a man and cut his ear off, and the dog got it. Been back here ever since. Ah." While going about his day, O'Hair must put up with his wife's vegetarian problems, relaxes by playing his bass fiddle, which he affectionately calls Lena. And the story ends when he captures a bank robber accidentally.

REVIEW:

Motion Picture Herald

The comedic mannerisms of the veteran W.C. Fields, as he utilizes them in his comedy, are still highly effective. Suffice it to say that an audience at a Broadway house enjoyed him and the short to the full, being in a state of almost continuous laughter. As the local barber with a henpecking wife, Fields shaves his patrons with an iron hand, reduces a corpulent man to a mere shadow in his steam room and paddles his hugh bass violin in his idea of music. When a bank robber walks into the shop, Fields leaves in a hurry, then takes the credit for capturing him. He is wholly enjoyable, and this yarn gives him ample opportunity to display his wares.

INTERNATIONAL HOUSE

1933

CREDITS:

Produced and distributed by Paramount. Directed by Edward Sutherland. Screenplay by Francis Martin and Walter De Leon from a story by Lou Heifetz and Neil Brant. Music and lyrics by Ralph Rainger and Leo Robin. Photographed by Ernest Haller. Running time: 70 minutes.

SYNOPSIS:

The story is set in China, where Doctor Wong has perfected a television apparatus. Seeking to get from Shanghai to Wu-wu, Tommy Nash gets mixed up with Peggy Hopkins Joyce. Nash is really in love with Carol, but

With Peggy Hopkins Joyce   UNIVERSITY OF TEXAS

CAST:

Peggy Hopkins Joyce	Peggy Hopkins Joyce
Professor Quail	W.C. Fields
Tommy Nash	Stuart Erwin
Carol Fortescue	Sari Maritza
Doctor Burns	George Burns
Nurse Allen	Gracie Allen
General Petronovich	Bela Lugosi
Doctor Wong	Edmund Breese
Sir Mortimer Fortescue	Lumsden Hare
Hotel Manager	Franklin Pangborn
Herr von Baden	Harrison Greene
Serge Borsky	Henry Sedley
Inspector Sun	James Wong

and Sterling Holloway, Rudy Vallee, Colonel Stoopnagle and Budd, Cab Calloway and his Orchestra, Baby Rose Marie, Ernest Wood, Edwin Stanley, Clem Beauchamp, Norman Ainslee, Louis Vincenot, Bo-Ling, Etta Lee, Bo-Ching, and Lona Andre

he always acquires some childish disease—chicken pox or mumps—as he is about to marry her. His efforts to explain to Carol how he came to be associated with the colorful Peggy provide plenty of complications.

When Nash breaks out with a rash, International House, the hotel where everyone is staying, is quarantined. Into this setup lands the flying Professor Quail, who becomes involved with Peggy H. Joyce also. Joyce's jealous husband appears and chases Professor Quail, but Quail is able to escape in his plane with Peggy Joyce. Nash buys Wong's invention, and a happy, peaceful conclusion is brought about when Carol understands Nash's problems and accepts him for her husband.

REVIEWS:
Motion Picture Herald

Primarily it is a gag-inspired ribald comedy. Action and dialogue are fast and furious. But much of the double-meaning dialogue is of the ultra-risqué type that is apt to start censors on the warpath. Constructed along the lines of a mammoth vaudeville show, the motivating story often is sidetracked entirely to permit a lot of unrelated hokum comedy. The radio personalities are rung in by means of a television gag, with the exception of Burns and Allen, who run a close second to, if they do not top, W.C. Fields in fun creation.

William Troy in *The Nation*

It would be altogether flattering to ascribe an idea to the expensive splurge in which Paramount has indulged in *International House*. All that it may justly be said to possess is a setting, and this can hardly be seen for the accumulation of radio, vaudeville, and musical-comedy talent which has been gathered together in the hope of making the picture a popular successor to *42nd Street*.

W.C. Fields alone appears with enough regularity throughout to afford any continuous amusement; and it must be reported that Mr. Fields is not nearly so amusing as he once seemed to be on stage. The patter with which he is supplied is thin and a little decayed, and he depends rather too much on mechanical aids to lift his comedy very far above the old Keystone level. Certain bits in the delicatessen fare which *International House* offers—Baby Marie's rendition of a very much grown-up "torch song," for example—are positively distressing, and the effect of the whole is to make one wonder whether Hollywood is not sinking beneath its own worst level in turning out such a picture as this.

Peggy Hopkins Joyce, Stuart Erwin, George Burns, and Gracie Allen

TILLIE AND GUS

1933

CREDITS:

Produced and distributed by Paramount. Directed by Francis Martin. Produced by Douglas MacLean. Screenplay by Walter DeLeon and Francis Martin from an original story by Rupert Hughes. Photographed by Benjamin Reynolds. Art direction by Hans Dreier and Harry Oliver. Running time: 58 minutes.

With Alison Skipworth

CAST:

Augustus Winterbottom	W.C. Fields
Tillie Winterbottom	Alison Skipworth
The "King"	Baby LeRoy
Mary Sheridan	Jacqueline Wells
Tom Sheridan	Clifford Jones
Phineas Pratt	Clarence Wilson
Captain Fogg	George Barbier
Commissioner McLennan	Barton MacLane
Judge	Edgar Kennedy
Defense Attorney	Robert McKenzie
Harrington	Master Williams

With Baby LeRoy and Alison Skipworth

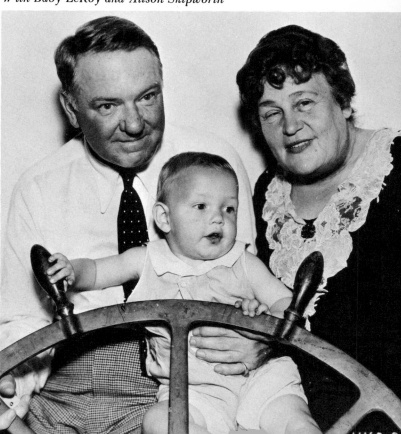

With Alison Skipworth

SYNOPSIS:

Phineas Pratt, a crooked lawyer, is trying to do Mary and Tom Sheridan and their son, King, out of the inheritance of her father. Notified of the situation of the estate are the girl's aunt, Tillie Winterbottom, plying her business at Tillie's Place, which is supposedly somewhere in China. Augustus Winterbottom, a professional card player, is asked to leave Alaska within the hour after a card game has gone wrong. The family believes the Winterbottoms to be missionaries. Augustus and Tillie meet accidentally on the train, take a few card sharps en route. Upon arrival they find Phineas Pratt trying to do the children out of a ferry franchise and an old broken-down boat. The only chance to retain the franchise is to win a victory over a rival boat, belonging to Pratt. The race is run and the Sheridan boat is the winner, and thus the franchise is saved, and all ends happily.

REVIEW:

Mordaunt Hall in *The New York Times*

Insane as are the doings in this concoction, they succeed in being really funny. It is the sort of thing admirably suited to Mr. Fields' peculiar genius. Miss Skipworth rivals Mr. Fields in arousing laughter.

ALICE IN WONDERLAND

1933

CREDITS:

Produced and distributed by Paramount. Directed by Norman McLeod. Screenplay by Joseph L. Mankiewicz and William Cameron Menzies from original material by Lewis Carrol. Music by Dmitri Tiomkin. Musical supervision by Nathaniel Finsten. Technical effects by Gordon Jennings and Farciot Edouart. Masks and costumes by Wally Westmore and Newt Jones. Settings by Robert Odell. Photographed by Henry Sharp and Bert Glennon. Editor: Edward Hoagland. Sound by Eugene Merritt. Running time: 90 minutes.

CAST:

Alice	Charlotte Henry
Cheshire Cat	Richard Arlen
Fish	Roscoe Ates
Gryphon	William Austin
White Knight	Gary Cooper
Leg of Mutton	Jack Duffy
Uncle Gilbert	Leon Errol
White Queen	Louise Fazenda
Humpty Dumpty	W.C. Fields
King of Hearts	Alec B. Francis
White Rabbit	Skeets Gallagher
Mock Turtle	Cary Grant
Cook	Lillian Harmer
Mouse	Raymond Hatton
Frog	Sterling Holloway
Mad Hatter	Edward Everett Horton
Tweedledee	Roscoe Karns
Joker	Baby LeRoy
Father William's Son	Lucien Littlefield
Sheep	Mae Marsh
Dodo Bird	Polly Moran
Tweedledum	Jack Oakie
Red Queen	Edna May Oliver
Plumb Pudding	George Ovey
Queen of Hearts	May Robson
March Hare	Charlie Ruggles
Dormouse	Jackie Searle
Duchess	Alison Skipworth
Caterpillar	Ned Sparks

and Ford Sterling, Jacqueline Wells, Billy Barty, Billy Bevan, Colin Campbell, Harvey Clark, Henry Ekezian, Meyer Grace, Ethel Griffies, Colin Kenny, Charles McNaughton, Patsy O'Byrne, Will Stanton, and Joe Torillo

SYNOPSIS:

Alice, while reading on a summer afternoon, sees a White Rabbit run across the lawn and disappear into a hole. She follows the Rabbit, falls into the hole, and finds herself in a beautiful garden. Here she goes through such experiences as growing smaller, growing larger, swimming in a pool of her tears, running a race, and talking about many things to many strange animals. She is led to the house of the Duchess, and when she tries to save a baby from the messy house, it turns into a pig and runs away. She goes on, meeting the Cheshire Cat who keeps disappearing and reappearing. Finally coming to the Mad Hatter's Tea Party, which she finds in confusion and which she cannot seem to help put in order, she runs away as soon as she can escape from it. Next she comes to a garden of talking flowers and here she meets the dreadful Queen, who leads her into other adventures. Finally Alice and the Queen arrive at a trial, where Alice causes confusion by knocking over the jury box. After attempting to set things right, Alice is asked to testify at the trial. But when Alice explains she knows nothing about the case, the Queen becomes very angry and says she will have Alice's head cut off. Alice, frightened, calls the Queen and her Court a pack of cards, and as the cards rush at her, she wakes up from the dream she has had.

REVIEWS:

Newsweek

The screen version of *Alice in Wonderland* is not likely to please either lovers of Lewis Carroll's famous book or those who like their cinema straight.

The story of the candid little girl who goes through a looking glass and meets a very odd collection of beings is closely adhered to. Scenarists have used incidents from both *Alice in Wonderland* and *Through The Looking Glass*. But they have been faithful to the author's spirit in somewhat lumbering fashion.

Included in the cast are Richard Arlen, Edna May Oliver, Polly Moran, Jack Oakie, Gary Cooper, W.C. Fields, May Robson, and Baby LeRoy—to name only a few highly publicized stars. With the exception of Miss Oliver and Baby LeRoy, their make-ups as the Cheshire

As Humpty-Dumpty

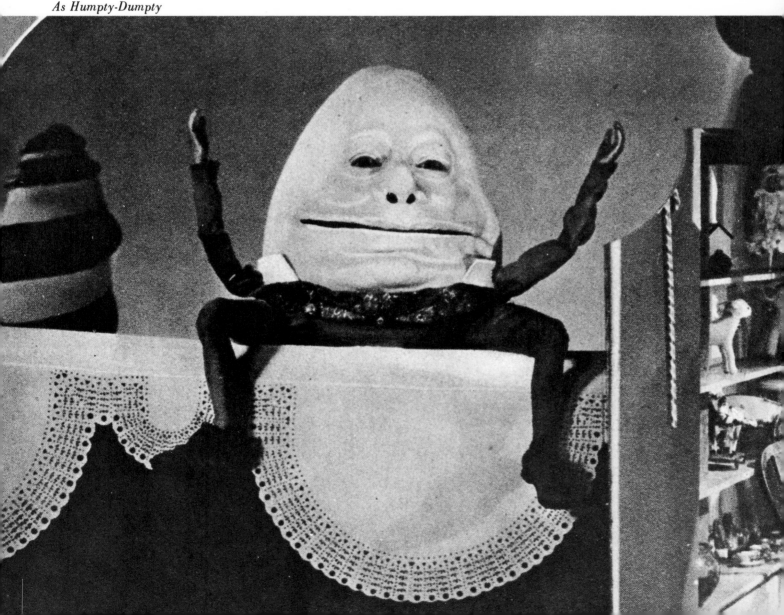

Cat, Tweedledum, the White Knight, Humpty Dumpty, and so on are so complete as to make them virtually unrecognizable.

Alice is played by Charlotte Henry of Brooklyn, New York, who heretofore has filled only small parts on the stage and screen. At 18 she seems still unsophisticated and quite in the spirit of the literary Alice. The only flaw in her portrayal is that the supposedly 12-year-old Alice has carefully plucked eyebrows.

The basic fault in the whole affair is that the constant repetition of cinematic miracles becomes monotonous. In the book one of the chief charms was the stimulation given to the imagination. In the film, they are only trick photography.

Argus in *The Literary Digest*

At first glance *Alice in Wonderland* and *Going Hollywood* would appear to have nothing in common, but both of these new products of the West Coast studios suffer from the same complaint. Superficially handsome, staged with lavish care and fairly bristling with celebrated performers, they represent an obsession with physical production which quite overshadows the material inherent in them. As a series of animated illustrations for Lewis Carroll's book in the Tenniel manner, *Alice in Wonderland* is a splendid success, but it achieves little more than this. Settings, costume, make-up and the distortion of backgrounds are perfectly executed. The characters, however, instead of being delightfully mad creatures engaged in one of the greatest fantasies ever conceived, move woodenly from one pose to another. Technically, the film

is excellent, translating all of the Carroll concepts to the screen in literal terms, the walrus and the carpenter episode being done as an animated cartoon. But although such notables as Gary Cooper, Edna May Oliver, W.C. Fields, Richard Arlen, Polly Moran and Alison Skipworth don strange disguises in the principal roles, they do not succeed in capturing the elusive and splendid quality of the book. A virtual newcomer, Charlotte Henry, gives the best performance.

With Charlotte Henry as Alice
and Jack Oakie as Tweedledum

Sterling Holloway as the Frog, with Charlotte Henry

SIX OF A KIND

1934

CREDITS:

Produced and distributed by Paramount. Directed by Leo McCarey. Screenplay by Walter DeLeon and Harry Ruskin from an original story by Keene Thompson and Douglas MacLean. Music by Ralph Rainger. Photographed by Henry Sharp. Art direction by Hans Dreier and Robert Odell. Editor: LeRoy Stone. Sound: Eugene Merritt. Running time: 65 minutes.

SYNOPSIS:

Mr. and Mrs. J. Pinkham Whinney are planning a motor trip to Hollywood, Calif., for their second honeymoon. Mrs. Whinney advertises for a couple to accompany them and share expenses. Of course, it turns out to be George Edward and Gracie DeVore, with their tremendous great Dane.

A fellow clerk in J. Pinkham Whinney's bank has put fifty thousand dollars in the latter's suitcase, intending

CAST:

J. Pinkham Whinney	Charlie Ruggles
Flora Whinney	Mary Boland
Sheriff John Hoxley	W.C. Fields
George Edward	George Burns
Gracie DeVore	Gracie Allen
Mrs. K. Rumford	Alison Skipworth
Ferguson	Bradley Page
Trixie	Grace Bradley
Gillette	William J. Kelly
Sparks	James Burke
Steele	Dick Rush
Butch	Walter Long
Mike	Leo Willis
Joe	Lew Kelly
Tom	Alp P. James
Doctor Busby	Tammany Young

and Paul Tead, George Pearce, Verna D. Hillie, Florence Enright, William Augustin, Kathleen Burke, Irving Bacon, Phil Dunham, Marty Faust, Lee Phelps, and Neal Burns

to hold him up his first night on the road. But Gracie insists on going by another route, and it is not until they reach Nuggetville, Nev., that detectives are able to catch up with them.

Sheriff John Hoxley and Mrs. K. Rumford, the local innkeeper, collaborate on a hilarious arrest. However, J. Pinkham Whinney is finally cleared and the Whinneys' traveling companions wish themselves on another unsuspecting couple and travel on. Finally Mr. and Mrs. J. P. Whinney can have a moment alone.

REVIEWS:
Argus in *The Literary Digest*

Filmgoers who have the proper enthusiasm for the art of W.C. Fields should find *Six of a Kind* one of the cinema joys of the year. Since this mad and wildly merry screen farce likewise features the antics of such expert performers as Burns and Allen, Mary Boland, Alison Skipworth, and Charles Ruggles, it obviously has its decided merits for any admirer of the more amiably lunatic school of film comedy, but there is reason to believe that it is the Fields addicts who will get the most fun out of this film. W.C. Fields is one of the rarest and most original of American comedians. There is gusto and richness to everything he does, and a certain outrageous air of frayed and battered dignity that is utterly and completely distinctive. Nor is it entirely his appearance and manner that are responsible for the striking hilarity. In the recent film version of *Alice in Wonderland* he played the character of "Humpty-Dumpty" and even while completely encased in his eggshell he was the only player in the entire cast of stars that was able to create a vivid characterization by his voice alone. This strangely effective voice of his is particularly surprising in view of the fact that he began his theatrical career as a juggler and pantomimist.

Cy Caldwell in *New Outlook*

Here is good fun for everyone, and especially grand entertainment for those discerning cinema patrons who delight in the solemn insanities of that king of comedians, Mr. W.C. Fields. In this gloriously crazy picture he is the Sheriff of a Nevada town, playing his famous game of billiards, describing how he came to be called Honest John, and remarking that everything really pleasant is either illegal, immoral, or fattening. To me, a devout Fields fan, he is the star of the picture.

Motion Picture Herald

This is a carnival of nonsensical comedy. Rarely has this reporter seen a crowd so enthusiastic in the appreciation of screen amusement as was the preview audience. Clocking the laughs was impossible; they came so fast and furiously. There's fun in the basic story; there's more fun in the atmospheric specialties which embellish it.

Newsweek

As might be expected from such an assemblage it is madcap from beginning to end. *Six of a Kind* is fun for everybody.

YOU'RE TELLING ME

1934

CREDITS:

Produced and distributed by Paramount. Directed by Earle Kenton. Screenplay by Walter De Leon and Paul M. Jones from a story by Julian Street. Dialogue by J.P. McEvoy. Music by Arthur Johnston and lyrics by Sam Coslow. Photographed by Alfred Gilks. Art direction by Hans Dreier and Robert Odell. Editor: Otho Lovering. Sound: Earl S. Hayman. Running time: 66 minutes.

CAST:

Sam Bisbee	W.C. Fields
Pauline Bisbee	Joan Marsh
Bob Murchison	Larry "Buster" Crabbe
Princess Lescaboura	Adrienne Ames
Mrs. Bessie Bisbee	Louise Carter
Mrs. Murchison	Kathleen Howard
Doc Beebe	James B. "Pop" Kenton
Charlie Bogle	Robert McKenzie
President of Tire Co.	George Irving
Frobisher	Jerry Stewart
Mayor	Dell Henderson
Mrs. Price	Nora Cecil
Crabbe	George MacQuarrie
Gray	John M. Sullivan

and Vernon Dent, Alfred Delcambre, Tammany Young, Frederic Sullivan, William Robyns, Harold Berquist, Lee Phelps, Frank O'Connor, Florence Enright, Isabelle La Mal, Edward Le Saint, James C. Morton, Elise Cavanna, Billy Engle, George Ovey, Al Hart, Hal Craig, and Dorothy Bay

SYNOPSIS:

Sam Bisbee is the worry-ridden head of a family that lives on the wrong side of the tracks. In an attempt to support his family, he spends his time on several inventions, such as a keyhole finder for inebriated homecomers. His lovely daughter adds to the complications of life by falling in love with the son of the town's leading snob.

Just as matters reach their lowest pitch, Sam gets a letter from a rubber company asking for a demonstration of his latest invention, a puncture-proof tire. He hilariously drives his car to the company's office, and parks it in a nonparking zone. Later he proudly shoots bullets at the tires. But his car has been replaced by a police car, an exact replica. The tires go flat. In despair he catches a train for home, and decides to commit suicide.

He tries to take his iodine in a collapsible spoon of his own invention. When the spoon collapses, he decides to face life after all. Then he sees a beautiful princess with a bottle of iodine. Rushing into her compartment, he lectures her on the evils of suicide and flings away the iodine, which she wanted to put on her sore finger.

In the end, Sam, with the help of the princess, makes the social grade, opens a golf course, and receives a fortune for his tire.

With Joan Marsh and Larry "Buster" Crab

With Adrienne Ames

REVIEWS:

Argus in *The Literary Digest*

Adding a curiously convincing quality of pathos to his customary comic brilliance, W.C. Fields offers one of his finest performances in the new screen play called, for no particular reason, *You're Telling Me.* Since the film permits Mr. Fields to play a disreputable inventor of mad devices and gives him an opportunity to appear in almost every scene, it can be very definitely set down as one of the most hilarious and satisfying of the recent motion-pictures.

It is a pleasant enough little fable, of the popular type, celebrating the success saga of the town reprobate, who makes good. With Mr. Fields permitted to run free and wild throughout its plot manipulations, though, it somehow takes on the qualities of heart-warming delight. Probably only Mr. Fields, of all the comedians, including Chaplin, could make that scene of attempted suicide hilarious, but, in some magic way, he does perform the miracle.

Everything he does in *You're Telling Me* is funny. He is as hilarious when walking silently down the street, slightly under the influence of alcoholic liquor and swaying a little in the breeze, as he is in the midst of that celebrated golf game of his, which is one of the comedy classics of our time. In addition to being enormously funny, though, he is the creator of a real character. This fumbling but robust, shrewd but blundering fellow has a rich, hearty, racy quality of Dickensian magnitude. The new picture offers a full-length portrait of his talents and, on that score, alone, it would be worth attention. The comedy creations of the story merely go to provide an extra dividend for the film followers. The work virtually is a monolog for Mr. Fields, but there are helpful performances in the supporting roles.

Newsweek

W.C. Fields is back on the job of splitting sides with his lugubrious nonsense in his latest movie, *You're Telling Me.* The minor characters are all well cast and amusing, but the whole looney business is just an excuse to prove that W.C. Fields is one of the craziest comedians on earth.

THE OLD-FASHIONED WAY

1934

CREDITS:

Produced and distributed by Paramount. Produced by William LeBaron. Directed by William Beaudine. Screenplay by Garnett Weston and Jack Cunningham from an original story by Charles Bogle (W.C. Fields). Music by Harry Revel and lyrics by Mack Gordon. Photographed by Benjamin Reynolds. Art direction by John Goodman. Sound: P.G. Wisdom. Running time: 66 minutes.

CAST:

The Great McGonigle	W.C. Fields
Wally Livingston	Joe Morrison
Betty McGonigle	Judith Allen
Cleopatra Pepperday	Jan Duggan
Mrs. Wendelschaffer	Nora Cecil
Albert Wendelschaffer	Baby LeRoy
Dick Bronson	Jack Mulhall
Charles Lowell	Joe Mills
Bartley Neuville	Samuel Ethridge
Mother Mack	Emma Ray
Agatha Sprague	Ruth Marion

and Del Henderson, Clarence Wilson, Richard Carle, Otis Harlan, Tammany Young, Dorothy Ray, Oscar Smith, Maxine Elliott Hicks, Lew Kelly, Davidson Clark, and Edward Le Saint

The Cast of *The Drunkard:*

Drover Stevens	Larry Grenier
Mary Wilson	Ruth Marion
Landlord of the Saloon	William Blatchford
William Dowton	Joe Morrison
Mr. Arden Rencelaw	Jeffrey Williams
Squire Cribbs	W.C. Fields
Edward Middleton (Drunkard)	Samuel Ethridge
Agnes Dowton	Judith Allen
The Minister	Donald Brown
The Villager	Tom Miller

With Judith Allen

SYNOPSIS:

The Great McGonigle and his troupe of thespians are playing the sticks in the gaslight era. However McGonigle must keep moving his troupe to avoid several sheriffs who are chasing him. In spite of his daughter Betty's romance with Wally Livingston, and the many difficulties with the members of his traveling show, McGonigle is able to keep one step ahead of each sheriff.

With Baby LeRoy

With Judith Allen and Joe Morrison

REVIEWS:

Andre Sennwald in *The New York Times*

To the lyric popping of vest buttons and the tortured noises of the laugh that begins deep down, the magnificent Mr. Fields has graciously placed himself on view at the Paramount Theater, and honest guffaws are once more heard on Forty-third Street. The great man, the omnipotent oom of one of the screen's most devoted cults, brings with him some new treasures, as well as a somewhat alarming collection of wheezes which, ten years ago in the vaudeville tank towns, must have seemed not long for this world. But somehow when Mr. Fields, in his necessary search for comic business, is forced to strike up a nodding acquaintance with vintage gags, they seem to become almost young again. There have been funnier Fields pictures, but the master himself, with his borrowed cigar, patrician cane, and medicine show clothes, is so much greater than his material that scarcely anything in which he appears can afford to be ignored by students of humor.

The New York Times

The vital statistics of this film could be imprisoned comfortably in a newspaper column. But historians, soiling their beards in moldy newspaper archives a century from now, would filch precious little on the history of the abdominal guffaw from that. What would it tell of the emotion that filled those of us who saw Mr. Fields boot Baby LeRoy in the rear with a pure classic motion that liberated the life-time frustrations of all males everywhere.

Mr. Fields' talents are continually being rediscovered. When he marches soberly in front of a camera, arranges his remarkably bulbous nose in the proper focus, attunes his dry nasal tones to the microphone, and gets down to the business of the day, he immediately becomes so devastating in his innocent onslaught on the funnybone that his helpless auditors are forced to conclude that so droll and resourceful a comic never faced an audience before.

Filming a scene from The Old-Fashioned Way

Golden Book Magazine

Then there's *The Old Fashioned Way* which has for its main appeal the one and only W.C. Fields, and his bag of tricks, consisting largely of the now famous juggling act and a foul-looking cigar. They've incorporated scenes from *The Drunkard* in this beautifully cock-eyed picture, and Fields plays the villainous role to the hilt. Somewhere along the line they have given Joe Morrison, who warbled *The Last Round Up* (remember?) all last summer everywhere and anywhere, a chance to sing a tune. They had to find some excuse to put him in there, didn't they? Fields, of course, has his troubles, with Baby LeRoy plaguing him, and a love-starved widow ditto. As a subway circuit Hamlet, he renounces manfully his daughter's love, so that she may go on to better things with the songbird of the western prairie, Joe. If you like high-class slapstick, you ought to look it up.

MRS. WIGGS OF THE CABBAGE PATCH

1934

CREDITS:

Produced and distributed by Paramount. Produced by Douglas MacLean. Directed by Norman Taurog. Screenplay by William Slavens McNutt and Jane Storm from an original story by Alice Hegan Rice and Anne Crawford Flexner. Photographed by Charles Lang. Art direction by Hans Dreier and Robert Odell. Running time: 80 minutes.

CAST:

Mrs. Wiggs	Pauline Lord
Mr. Stubbins	W.C. Fields
Miss Hazy	ZaSu Pitts
Lucy Olcott	Evalyn Venable
Bob Redding	Kent Taylor
Bagby	Charles Middleton
Mr. Wiggs	Donald Meek
Bill Wiggs	Jimmy Butler
Jimmy Wiggs	George Breakston
Australia Wiggs	Edith Fellows
Europena Wiggs	Virginia Weidler
Asia Wiggs	Carmencita Johnson

and George Reed, Mildred Gover, Arthur Housman, Walter Walker, Sam Flint, James Robinson, Bentley Hewlett, Edward Tamblin, Al Shaw, Sam Lee, Del Henderson, George Pearce, Lillian Elliott, and Earl Pingree

With ZaSu Pitts

SYNOPSIS:

In their patchwork shack on the "wrong side" of the railroad tracks, Mrs. Wiggs and her five children—Billy, Australia, Asia, Europena, and Jimmy—and the dog Klondike are getting a double Thanksgiving Day thrill.

First, Billy adopts a worn-out old workhorse, which an itinerant dealer has given up for useless, and the whole family, Mrs. Wiggs in the lead, turns out to save the animal. Secondly, while the Wiggses are preparing to give thanks for a meager meal of leftover stew, Miss Lucy, from one of the "big houses," brings them a real Thanksgiving Day feast. The Wiggses are truly happy, the only cloud on their horizon being the absence of Mr. Wiggs, who five years ago, "thunk" himself into taking a long journey and has never been heard from since. The Wiggses invite their neighbor, Miss Hazy, to join them.

Miss Lucy's troubles are introduced into the Wiggses' home by a visit from Bob Redding, a young newspaper editor and Miss Lucy's fiance. Lucy and Bob are in the midst of a lover's quarrel but Bob, on his visit, notices Jimmy's bad cough and makes arrangements to have him sent to the hospital for treatment.

With the horse Cuby, Billy Wiggs, the main support of the Wiggs family, peddles kindling wood and works up quite a business. The most successful deal he has ever put across results in the trading of a load of wood for five tickets to a show. During the performance, while the Wiggses are having a hilarious time, Mrs. Wiggs is called to the hospital. She is just in time to be with Jimmy when he dies.

But even this sad blow cannot quell the Wiggs family. Mrs. Wiggs sets out to secure a husband for Miss Hazy and Mr. Stubbins is brought into the circle of the Wiggs friends. Before marrying Miss Hazy, Stubbins demands a sample of her cooking, and Mrs. Wiggs arranges to help her friend pass the test by substituting her own dishes. Stubbins, delighted with the dishes Mrs. Wiggs has prepared, concludes the marriage pact. But Miss Hazy's happiness is short.

With ZaSu Pitts

With ZaSu Pitts

With ZaSu Pitts

Meanwhile, Bob Redding and Miss Lucy, realizing the need of the Wiggs family, set out to bring Mr. Wiggs back by advertising in newspapers all over the country. The need for Mr. Wiggs becomes acute when Bagby, who holds the mortgage to their home, announces that he will foreclose.

Suddenly, out of nowhere, appears Mr. Wiggs himself, the same meek, silent, thoughtful man, just as seedy-looking as ever, dressed in a hand-me-down suit. Although his appearance belies her hopes, Mrs. Wiggs anxiously goes through the pockets of the suit in the hope of finding twenty-five dollars to cover the mortgage —and, to the surprise of everyone, including Mr. Wiggs, she finds a neatly folded twenty-five dollars in one of the pockets.

Their home saved, the happy, reunited family turn out in gala array for the marriage of their good friends Miss Lucy and Mr. Bob.

REVIEWS:

Otis Ferguson in *The New Republic*

Mrs. Wiggs of the Cabbage Patch will do to illustrate a trend in humor that we might be happy to see the last of: it is in the smile-with-a-tear tradition, all so beastly clean and wholesome. Heroism in the face of obstacles. Obstacles in the face of heroism. Everything. Strangely enough, in execution it does not live up to the first reports, which said something about Mr. Taurog having to go around in a gas-mask from the first take, even its own director. Pauline Lord does as much as she can with Mrs. Wiggs, and that is quite a lot. ZaSu Pitts and W.C. Fields make their parts of it even enjoyable. But wrapped up in the center of everything is the main theme, which is vicious to just such an extent as it is made believable. A nasty all's-right-with-the-world burlesque of poverty, with emotions to tug at such heartstrings as are worn dangling from the mouth.

Reprinted by courtesy of Dorothy Chamberlain.

With ZaSu Pitts

Andre Sennwald in *The New York Times*

The cynics who fled down the streets upon being informed that Hollywood had taken up Mrs. Wiggs may now come back. Norman Taurog and his assistants have wrestled a surprising sum of merriment out of the tearful minor classic. To be sure, the shabby little woman with the shawl is still fussing over her geographically titled brood among the ramshackle cottages of the Cabbage Patch. But now there is Pauline Lord to take the sting of furious optimism out of it and to spice the sentimental brew with sly humor. The patient and doleful Miss Hazy has become the fluttering ZaSu Pitts and, for no more pious reason than to make you roar, she has been provided with a suitor in the outlandishly funny person of W.C. Fields, who, unfortunately, is brought onto the screen only in the last twenty minutes or so. All in all, *Mrs. Wiggs of the Cabbage Patch* has been bullied into a genuinely amusing carnival for this disrepectful year of grace.

With ZaSu Pitts

IT'S A GIFT

1934

CREDITS:

Distributed by Paramount. Produced by William Le-Baron. Directed by Norman McLeod. Screenplay by Jack Cunningham from an original story by Charles Bogle (W.C. Fields) and J.P. McEvoy. Photographed by Henry Sharp. Art direction by Hans Dreier and John B. Goodman. Sound: Earl S. Hayman. Running time: 73 minutes.

CAST:

Harold Bissonette	W.C. Fields
Mildred Bissonette	Jean Rouverol
John Durston	Julian Madison
Amelia Bissonette	Kathleen Howard
Norman Bissonette	Tom Bupp
Everett Ricks	Tammany Young
Baby Dunk	Baby LeRoy
Jasper Fitchmueller	Morgan Wallace
Mr. Muckle	Charles Sellon
Mrs. Dunk	Josephine Whittell
Miss Dunk	Diana Lewis

and T. Roy Barnes, Spencer Charters, Guy Usher, Del Henderson, Jerry Mandy, James Burke, William Tooker, Edith Kingdon, Patsy O'Byrne, and Billy Engle

SYNOPSIS:

Mr. Bissonette is the bumbling proprietor of a small-town general store, as well as the helpless victim of a shrewish wife. The fumbling Mr. Bissonette is badgered and hounded beyond his generous powers of endurance by customers and relatives. Finally he buys an orange ranch through the mail. Then he boards a rattletrap fliv-ver with his wife, his daughter Mildred and her fiance, John Durston, a salesman, and sets off across the country to California. The money for the ranch and trip were provided by Mr. Bissonette's late uncle, who left his money to his nephew. When he arrives, he discovers the orange grove is a section of sunbaked desert land with a shack on it, situated between other orange groves.

However a promoter wants his land for a racetrack, so Bissonette sells it for forty thousand dollars and is thus able to buy himself a real orange grove to settle down on.

REVIEWS:

Andre Sennwald in *The New York Times*

Perhaps if the W.C. Fields idolators continue their campaign on his behalf over a sufficient period of years his employers may finally invest him with a production befitting his dignity as a great artist. In the meantime such comparatively journeyman pieces as *It's a Gift* will serve very adequately to keep his public satisfied.

With the one exception of Charlie Chaplin, there is nobody but Mr. Fields who could manage the episode with the blind and deaf man in the store so as to make it funny instead of just a trifle revolting.

Argus in *The Literary Digest*

Listed among the authors of the new W.C. Fields vehicle, *It's a Gift,* will be found the name of one Charles Bogle. One given to bets on such things might be willing to wager that there never was anyone named Charles Bogle, and the chances are that he would be right. For, according to reports from Hollywood, the lyric Bogle is no less a person than the antic Mr. Fields himself, hiding his literary light under a penname. In *It's a Gift,* the modest author has been wise enough to create a role permitting the great Fields to appear in virtually every scene, and to turn its plot into a veritable monolog for the funniest comedian of them all.

Thanks to the fact that the film provides a field-day for the star, it is an enormously amusing succession of rough-and-ready "gags."

Nevertheless, it is about time that the Fields enthusiasts got together and demanded that their hero have a production worthy of him. *It's a Gift* looks as though it had taken two days to make, had cost $100, and had been photographed with one of the early Biograph cameras.

It is crude, clumsy, and quite amateurish in its appearance. It merely happens that a great comedian appears in it and has a free hand in his brilliant clowning, with the result that the defects become unimportant, and the film emerges as a comedy delight. Just for a change, though, a skillful production might be accorded Mr. Fields, just to see what the effect would be.

DAVID COPPERFIELD

1935

CREDITS:

Produced and distributed by Metro-Goldwyn-Mayer. Produced by David O. Selznick. Directed by George Cukor. Screenplay by Howard Estabrook from the novel by Charles Dickens. Adaptation by Hugh Walpole. Musical score by Herbert Stothart. Photographed by Oliver T. Marsh. Art direction by Cedric Gibbons. Wardrobe by Dolly Tree. Editor: Robert J. Kern. Special effects by Slavko Vorkapich. Running time: 133 minutes.

With Freddie Bartholomew

CAST:

Micawber	W.C. Fields
Dan Peggotty	Lionel Barrymore
Dora Spenlow	Maureen O'Sullivan
Agnes Wickfield	Madge Evans
Aunt Betsy	Edna May Oliver
Mr. Wickfield	Lewis Stone
David, the Child	Freddie Bartholomew
David, the Man	Frank Lawton
Mrs. Clara Copperfield	Elizabeth Allan
Uriah Heep	Roland Young
Mr. Murdstone	Basil Rathbone
Clickett	Elsa Lanchester
Mrs. Micawber	Jean Cadell
Nurse Peggotty	Jessie Ralph
Mr. Dick	Lennox Pawle
Jane Murdstone	Violet Kemble-Cooper
Mrs. Gummidge	Una O'Connor
Ham	John Buckler
Steerforth	Hugh Williams
Limmiter	Ivan Simpson
Barkis	Herbert Mundin
Little Em'ly, the Child	Fay Chaldecott
Little Em'ly, the Woman	Florine McKinney
Agnes, the Child	Marilyn Knowlden
Dr. Chillip	Harry Beresford
Mary Ann	Mabel Colcord
The Vicar	Hugh Walpole
Janet	Renee Gadd

SYNOPSIS:

David is born six months after his father's death, and his mother Clara Copperfield attempts to rear him. To improve her widow's lot, she marries a Mr. Murdstone, who turns out to be a cruel stepfather. Mr. Murdstone often mistreats David and finally has him sent to a boarding school. But David's mother dies, and he has to return home to work in his stepfather's export warehouse. It is at this time that David first meets Mr. Micawber at whose place he stays. Mr. Micawber soon leaves to go to debtor's prison. Later David runs away to Dover to live with his Great Aunt Betsy. Mr. Murdstone and his sister attempt to take David back, but Aunt Betsy, with Mr. Dick's advice, keeps David and turns the angry Murdstones away. David returns to school. Then he meets Agnes Wickfield, who involves him in her father's business problems with Uriah Heep and Mr. Steerforth. David helps expose these two, and leaves Agnes to marry Dora Spenlow, who remains a very childish wife. However, the sickly Dora dies, and Agnes and David are brought together again.

With Freddie Bartholomew

With Freddie Bartholomew and Jean Cadell

With Jean Cadell, Freddie Bartholomew, and Elsa Lanchester

REVIEWS:

William Troy in *The Nation*

It must immediately be acknowledged that Hollywood has spared no expense in providing for its audience the desired emotion of recognition. From W.C. Fields to Hugh Walpole the players in the film have been recruited from the very front ranks of contemporary entertainers. And on the whole the cast is as competent as it is expensive. The greatest single inspiration was the choice of Frank Lawton, perhaps the most satisfactory juvenile on the English-speaking stage at the moment, for the title role. So naturally does this young actor fall into sincerity in his rendition of the emotions that he very nearly forgets that he is playing Dickens. He almost destroys the illusion that everybody else is building up. A less happy selection was made in the case of Master Freddie Bartholomew (as David the Child), who seemed to this spectator too effeminate and at times badly trained in the use of his voice. Concerning W.C. Fields' Micawber opinion is certain to be very much divided. Although

it may be granted that he conforms to the physical image remarkably well, he will probably be found lacking in sufficient gusto in his more important scenes. Here especially is a case where a less well-known actor would have worked against fewer handicaps in the audience's recollection. And the same is true for Roland Young, who is fundamentally too charming an actor to be properly sinister in the role of Uriah Heep. The less well-known players do, as a matter of fact, come off very much better; the Mrs. Micawber, the Peggotty, and the Steerforth are excellent; and for this reviewer at least, the actor who plays the last-named evokes the early Victorian period more uncannily than anyone else in the film. In brief, Hollywood has taken no chances in doing justice to the favorite author of G.K. Chesterton, Hugh Walpole, and Alexander Woollcott; and the result is another of those large-scale debauches in nineteenth-century sentimentalism which will one day swell the archives of early twentieth-century evasion.

The Literary Digest

A beautiful, heart-warming and completely satisfying motion picture has been made out of the vast and magnificent bulk of *David Copperfield*. It seems likely that never has so accurate a screen version, in spirit, story, and characterization, been arranged from a long and demanding novel. In at least one case a certain amount of plot-telescoping has been done—David goes to but one school. At least one reasonably important minor character—the gentle and kindly Traddles—has been forgotten altogether.

Only the most captious observer or the most pedantic of Dickens-lovers, however, could bother about such minor inaccuracies, for the film, running for more than two hours, manages to do everything in the most complete fashion which could be sensibly demanded, and the work becomes one of the most delightful of adaptations.

In this limited space it should be enough to mention the work of the actors—all of whom seem to have stepped out of the drawings of Phiz and come immediately to dramatic life. A handsome and sensitive boy named Freddie Bartholomew is a perfect picture of David the boy. When time comes for him to grow up it is amazing to see the man-sized David played by Frank Lawton, an able young actor, who looks astonishingly like Freddie Bartholomew at the age of twenty.

W.C. Fields is a magnificent Micawber, reminding all that he is a grand actor as well as the funniest of comedians.

With Freddie Bartholomew

With Frank Lawton and Jean Cadell

With Frank Lawton and Roland Young

Grenville Vernon in *Commonweal*

It is evident that at last the possibilities of Dickens are being recognized by the magnates who control the destinies of the screen. Only recently they gave us *Great Expectations*; now they have given us *David Copperfield*. It is of course impossible to put the great panorama of a Dickens novel in its full richness into a bare two hours; either the story or the characters must be sacrificed, and in a work of the length and richness of *David Copperfield* this is peculiarly true. Yet in this adaptation by Hugh Walpole and Howard Estabrook the story has been retained, and the characters are not neglected. I, for one, should have liked more of Mr. Micawber and slightly less of Mr. Peggotty, but on the whole the balance is pretty well preserved. The action is leisurely; if it were not, it would have been false to Dickens, and a Dickens film

with Dickens absent beggars the imagination! So we have Dickens unjazzed which shows that the movies are beginning to come of age. And, best of all, the players chosen to present the film are on the whole excellent. First honors must go to Freddie Bartholomew, who portrays David, the child. This little English boy's performance is one of the most sensitive and touching evocations of a child that either the screen or the stage has seen, a veritable little masterpiece. And almost equally good is Frank Lawton's David grown up. He looks startlingly like the boy David and plays his part with sincerity and poignancy. W.C. Fields looks Micawber, but his enunciation is far from distinct, which lessens the flamboyancy of the character. Roland Young gives a finely etched portrait of Uriah Heep and Edna May Oliver almost as fine a one as Aunt Betsy.

With Frank Lawton and Jean Cadell

Martin Herne in *The London Mercury*

The production of *David Copperfield* at Hollywood was no ordinary event. The directors of Metro-Goldwyn-Mayer knew that an Englishman who criticizes Dickens might as well confess at once that he is on the side of atheism, free love, and the destruction of the British Empire. They knew, also, that the "purity campaign" in America, was too strong to be ignored. They needed good marks; and they saw a chance of earning good marks and good revenue by treating Dickens with tremendous and well-advertised respect.

In spite of the many weaknesses, however, the film is sure of success, for most people will chiefly want to see the familiar characters, and here they are, nearly all of them, well acted and reasonably life-like. The Micawber of W.C. Fields has the right fruity flavor, but a comedian accustomed to American dialogue is bound to have trouble with Micawber's rolling periods. I wonder what Charles Laughton, who was offered the part of Micawber, would have made of it? He refused, apparently, because he was afraid he would not be amusing enough.

With Frank Lawton and Roland Young

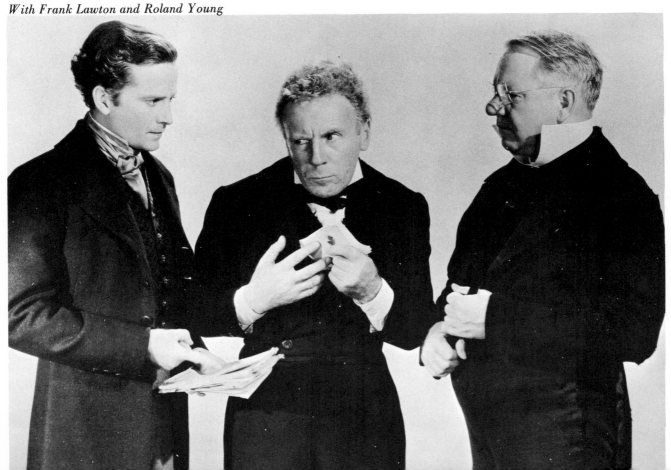

MISSISSIPPI

1935

CREDITS:

Produced and distributed by Paramount. Produced by Arthur Hornblow, Jr. Directed by Edward A. Sutherland. Adapted by Herbert Fields and Claude Binyon from an original story by Booth Tarkington. Screenplay by Francis Martin and Jack Cunningham. Music by Richard Rodgers and lyrics by Lorenz Hart. Photographed by Charles Lang. Art direction by Hans Dreier and Bernard Herzburn. Editor: Chandler House. Sound: Eugene Merritt. Running time: 80 minutes.

CAST:

Tom Grayson	Bing Crosby
Commodore Jackson	W.C. Fields
Lucy Rumford	Joan Bennett
Alabam'	Queenie Smith
Elvira Rumford	Gail Patrick
General Rumford	Claude Gillingwater, Sr.
Major Patterson	John Miljan
Joe Patterson	Edward Pawley
Captain Blackie	Fred Kohler, Sr.
Cabin Kids	Five Cabin Kids
Rumbo	John Larkin
Lavinia	Libby Taylor
Miss Markham	Theresa Maxwell Conover
Hefty	Paul Hurst

and Harry Meyers, Charles L. King, Jean Rouverol, Ann Sheridan, Mildred Stone, Mary Ellen Brown, Eddie Sturgis, George Lloyd, Al Richmond, J. P. McGowan, Francis McDonald, Stanley Andrews, Harry Cody, Clarence Geldert, Forrest Taylor, Mabel Van Buren, Bill Harwood, Jack Mulhall, Jack Carlyle, Richard Scott, Arthur Millett, Clarence L.

Sherwood, Bert Lindley, Fred (Snowflake) Toone, Roy Bailey, James Burke, Jan Duggan, King Baggott, Mahlon Hamilton, Jules Cowles, Bruce Covington, Warren Rogers, Dan Crimmins, William Howard Gould, Jean Clarendon, Lew Kelly, Matthew Betz, and Warner Richmond

With Bing Crosby

SYNOPSIS:

The story opens aboard the riverboat where Commodore Jackson is amusing his clients, but soon shifts to the plantation where Tom Grayson is on the spot at his engagement party to Elvira Rumford because he refuses to fight a duel with fire-eating Major Patterson, a fanatic exponent of the *code duello*, as a means of satisfying imaginary outrages against his honor. Branded as a coward by General Rumford and his daughter Elvira, Tom leaves and joins the showboat. However, Elvira's younger sister, Lucy Rumford, looks upon Tom as a hero and is saddened by his departure.

The Commodore exploits Tom as "the singing killer," a phony reputation which takes on literal significance

With Joan Bennett and Gail Patrick

when, engaged in a wild brawl with rowdy Captain Blackie, that worthy accidentally kills himself. Lucy, pining for her absent lover, is at a school, but the girls, taking a vacation, come to the spot where the showboat is docked. The Commodore has billed Tom as the killer of a southern gentleman who happened to be Lucy's cousin. Of course, when Lucy discovers that it is Tom, she is angered and her love turns to abhorrence. Suddenly Tom acts the character the phony buildup has given him and he invades the Rumford mansion; after beating up Major Patterson and his equally tough brother, he leaves them cringing in terror. Then he breaks down the door of Lucy's room and carries her off to the showboat where, with the Commodore's help, he explains that his fearsome reputation is only a myth. Lucy is overjoyed and embraces Tom happily as the story ends.

Joan Bennett and Bing Crosby

With Bing Crosby

REVIEWS:

Andre Sennwald in *The New York Times*

Amid an atmosphere of magnolia, crinoline and Kentucky whiskey, the boozy genius of Mr. Fields and the subterranean croon of Mr. Crosby strike a happy compromise in *Mississippi*. Having its money on Mr. Fields, this column considered the photoplay pleasant only when he was around.

McCarthy in *Motion Picture Herald*

For entertainment and showmanship purposes this attraction offers W.C. Fields and his comedy, Bing Crosby and his crooning, and for a story content a muchly altered and sometimes satiric picturization of Booth Tarkington's novel originally titled *The Fighting Coward*. The result is a melodramatic and sometimes tense romance. Fields' comedy, in both dialogue and action, is good for its full quota of laughs. Songs which Crosby sings are "Down by the River," "Soon" and "It's Easy to Remember," plus his own version of "Swanee River" with Negro choral accompaniment.

Variety

Paramount obviously couldn't make up its mind what it wanted to do with the film; it's rambling and hokey. For a few minutes it's sheer farce, for a few moments it's romance. And it never jells. Viewing in New York suggests that it may have been severely cut after completion because some bits and sequences are not even followed through, but left in the air.

The story comes off the shelf. It was produced at least twice previously; first silent entitled *The Fighting Coward* and next as a talker for Buddy Rogers under its stage title *Magnolia*. This time it has been completely written over, but gagged up too much. Some of the lines are funny, but that isn't enough. Fields works hard throughout the film and saves it, giving it whatever entertainment value it has.

With Bing Crosby

THE MAN ON THE FLYING TRAPEZE

1935

CREDITS:

Produced and distributed by Paramount. Produced by William LeBaron. Directed by Clyde Bruckman. Screenplay by Ray Harris, Sam Hardy, Jack Cunningham, and Bobby Vernon from an original story by Charles Bogle (W.C. Fields) and Sam Hardy. Photographed by Al Gilks. Editor: Richard Currier. Running time: 65 minutes.

CAST:

Ambrose Wolfinger	W.C. Fields
Hope Wolfinger	Mary Brian
Leona Wolfinger	Kathleen Howard
Claude Bensinger	Grady Sutton
Mrs. Bensinger	Vera Lewis
Mr. Peabody	Lucien Littlefield
President Malloy	Oscar Apfel
Adolph Berg	Lew Kelly
"Willie," the Weasel	Tammany Young
"Legs" Garnett	Walter Brennan
Night Court Judge	Arthur Aylesworth
Mishabbob	Harry Ekezian
Tosoff	Tor Johnson
T.P. Wallaby	David Clyde

and Mickey Bennett, Dorothy Thompson, Lorin Baker, Pat O'Malley, Sarah Edwards, James Flavin, Robert Littlefield, Michael S. Visaroff, Charles Morris, Eddie Sturgis, Eddie Chandler, Edward Gargan, James Burke, Joseph Sauers, Mickey McMasters, Keith Daniels, Sam Lufkin, Billy Bletcher, Helen Dickson, Albert Taylor, Jack Baxley, George French, Carlotta Monti, Harry C. Bradley, and Rosemary Theby

SYNOPSIS:

The hero is Ambrose Wolfinger, a crestfallen, fantastically good-natured householder, who is surrounded by a shrewish second wife, a mother-in-law, a lazy, unpleasant brother-in-law, and a daughter by a first marriage. He makes applejack in his cellar, which one night is invaded by burglars; they get tipsy and start to sing. When Mrs. Wolfinger wakes Ambrose and orders him to investigate, he inquires, "What are they singing?" He goes to the cellar to investigate and joins the burglars in a round of drinks.

Ambrose Wolfinger is useful to his employer because he remembers every foible and family tie of important clients; he is almost impossible to fire because in his confused files no one but he can find anything. To get his first afternoon off in twenty-five years to go to a wrestling match, he tells his boss that he must attend his mother-in-law's funeral. Delayed by a sarcastic traffic policeman, a truculent chauffeur and a runaway tire, he reaches the match just in time to be felled by the flying form of a wrestler who has been thrown not only out of the ring but out of the building. Battered, he reaches home to find his mother-in-law story taken so

With Kathleen Howard

With Mary Brian

With Kathleen Howard and Mary Brian

seriously that the house is full of floral tributes and newspaper headlines ascribe the death to poisoned liquor. An abrupt reversal of the situation, started by Ambrose's powerful punch to his brother-in-law's jaw, ends with his one-time tormentors in utter subjugation and Ambrose enjoying a raise in pay and a four weeks' vacation.

REVIEWS:

The Literary Digest

At fifty-six, W.C. Fields has reached the golden strands of Hollywood as a star in his own earned right. His pictures already follow a pattern: the dialog written for him is rarely above average; plot is never taxing to the mind; and he is doomed to be the misunderstood but lovable father. But schooled in the art of pantomime, yet possessing complete mastery over his voice, endowed by nature with a countenance able to portray the slightest trace of injured dignity or treasured momentary victory, his mere presence on the screen tickles the humor of his own particular audience.

Somewhat tedious in spots and completely unpretentious, the picture is a straight role for the character Fields has made his own—a man of family, oppressed by the world and domesticity, who courageously maintains a semblance of dignity.

Time

    Man on the Flying Trapeze will please those Fields cultists who are satisfied if that excellent comedian is visible and audible almost all the time.

With Kathleen Howard

With Kathleen Howard

POPPY

1936

CREDITS:

Produced and distributed by Paramount. Produced by William LeBaron. Associate producer: Paul Jones. Directed by A. Edward Sutherland. Assistant director: Richard Harlan. Screenplay by Waldemar Young and Virginia Van Upp from a play by Dorothy Donnelly. Music and lyrics by Ralph Rainger and Leo Robin, and Sam Coslow and Frederick Hollander. Costumes by Edith Head. Photographed by William Mellor. Art direction by Hans Dreier and Bernard Herzburn. Film editor: Stuart Heisler. Sound: Earl S. Hayman. Running time: 75 minutes.

With Rochelle Hudson

CAST:

Professor Eustace McGargle	W.C. Fields
Poppy	Rochelle Hudson
Billy Farnsworth	Richard Cromwell
Mayor Farnsworth	Granville Bates
Countess Maggie Tubbs DePuizzi	Catherine Doucet
Attorney Whiffen	Lynne Overman
Sarah Tucker	Maude Eburne
Egmont	Bill Wolfe
Constable Bowman	Adrian Morris
Frances Parker	Rosalind Keith

and Ralph M. Remley, Wade Boteler, Tom Herbert, Cyril Ring, Jack Baxley, Harry Wagner, Frank Sully, Eddie C. Waller, Dell Henderson, Tammany Young, Dewey Robinson, Tom Kennedy, Nora Cecil, Gertrude Sutton, Grace Goodall, Ada May Moore, Jerry Bergen, Doc Sone, Malcolm Waite, Dick Rush, and Charles McMurphy

SYNOPSIS:

As a happy-go-lucky drifter, Professor McGargle, accompanied by his daughter, arrives in a country town. Quickly the Professor establishes himself as the prize medicine-selling star of a traveling carnival. Meanwhile his daughter Poppy meets and falls in love with Mayor Farnsworth's son Billy. The charm of this is balanced by the menace to the Professor of gabby Countess De-Puizzi, masquerading as heir to the Putnam estates and fortunes. In connivance with a hick lawyer, Whiffen, the Professor sets Poppy up as a claimant for the estate, convincing the Mayor-executor that she is the legitimate heir.

But Poppy encounters romantic troubles with Billy and some that threaten to be more serious crop up for the Professor as Whiffen, teaming up with the Countess, introduces a double-cross. As things look dangerous to both, kindly Sarah Tucker, who has befriended Poppy, recognizes the resemblance between the child and the deceased Mrs. Putnam.

Forced to make a clean breast of his history, the Professor tells how he had adopted Poppy years ago and that he knew all along that she was the rightful claimant. This dismays Whiffen and the Countess, who is now revealed as a showgirl. The finale is thus a happy ending for the Professor, Poppy, and Billy.

With Lynne Overman

With Lynne Overman and Granville Bates

REVIEWS:

Alistair Cooke in *The Listener*

He wanders through small shops and circuses, public bars, children, sideshows, straw hats and nagging women with a bemused aloofness that makes him in this life but not of it. He's Bacchus dropped from the clouds and made to work in the corner grocer's. He has every decent human motive and would almost choose to act out an honest life, but around him he sees small-timers cheating each other all the way. That wouldn't distress him either if there was any style to their tricks. But people are so mean and clumsy he feels obliged to give them a lesson or two, an accomplished robbery here, a short bargain there, done with enough flourish to give the human game some dignity. He'll try any roguery once, just to feel the thrill of the gestures, just to feel superior to the morons who suspect him. But he never hopes to win anything. Except at the end of the film he does. It has been Fields' great and individual improvement on the Chaplin pathetic ne'er-do-well that instead of fading away up a lonely road poor but blithe, he ends by winning decisively for the first time in his life.

In *It's a Gift* he goes through endless squabbling failures to get across the continent and claim an orange grove that turns out to be a shambles. But a man comes along and offers him a fortune for the land as a building site. And the last shot was Fields leaning back, in a seersucker suit and a neatly pinned tie, fanning himself in the sun and downing a highball. In *Poppy*, he begins promisingly by selling his talking dog and not unnaturally taking the voice away with him, but then after much intermediate wrangling with the poor fools ("Who

With Catherine Doucet

will be the next to outwit me? This is a game of chance")
he ends by going off with the Mayor's hat, rather silkier
than his own, and a fistful of the Mayor's cigars.

It was cruel that Mr. Bernard Shaw should be asking
for "better voices" and good diction on the screen the
week that Fields came along. For he stands as a con-
venient symbol of the war between the stage and screen,
between "fine speaking" and ordinary day-to-day think-
ing aloud. He plays with two voices—a smooth, pompous,
trained voice and a mumbling, bemused one. And, not to
take sides too openly, I should say he uses the first, the
overripe voice, for all his artifice, all the public occasions
when he's trying to swindle somebody or claim a family
tree. But he's always caught out by the second voice, by
his muttered suspicion that this sort of thing has happened before in the world's history. He may with a fine
flourish of hand and elbow say, "I have here, gentlemen,
a very fine timepiece that cost five hundred dollars, yes
sir, five hundred dollars," and you can hear him saying
under his breath, "you'll never get away with it."

Every time he tries to be an actor, horse sense whispers
in his ear. Every time his first voice tries to deceive other
people, his second is telling him out of the corner of his
mouth that he's kidding nobody but himself. It doesn't
matter much if you don't even catch what the second
voice is saying. It's simply nervous speech with, I'm
afraid, Mr. Shaw, definitely bad diction—it's Everyman's
misgivings, second thoughts, delayed humility. In *Poppy*,
it happens to be the language of W.C. Fields, an American juggler. Ideally, it's the common language of all
Cockneys, and French taxi-drivers, and Texas cattlemen,
and all simple men permanently impressed by the irony
of human dignity. It's a precious language that belongs
more to the movies than to any other form of deception.
For it's the phonetic equivalent of a sense of fact. And

On the set with director Edward Sutherland

when the screen takes Mr. Shaw's advice and doctors its
voice, it can say goodbye to most of the virtues the
screen can still claim over a theater resonant with a
clatter of consonants and coy scruples. I'll sit through
the movies just as long as the natural voice is accepted
as the standard. The day Gary Cooper gets busy with his
diction, I shall take to a tricycle.

With Irene Bennett (stand-in for Rochelle Hudson)

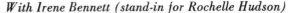

Waiting on the set with Catherine Doucet

The Hollywood Reporter
It is artful nonsense from a master of mad-waggery.

Hollywood Daily Variety
Slow and lacking smoothness, *Poppy* needs straightening out before it will please many other than out-and-out W.C. Fields fans.

With Granville Bates

With Rochelle Hudson and Granville Bates

With Ida Mae Moore

The Literary Digest

Poppy is the motion-picture W.C. Fields almost didn't make. It is the picture no other clown in Hollywood could have made.

Fields put his trade-mark on the role twenty years ago when he turned the jumble-shop stage show of the same name into a comedy triumph. Then he made a silent film version. The present talking-singing version is all that any Fields addict could ask.

When Paramount first considered the picture last winter, Fields didn't think he would live to see a camera turn; and he didn't care. Gravely ill, weak as a cat, the comedian went out to the desert; he spent weeks there letting the sun bake strength back into him.

When the picture started, he came back to town. Even then he told friends he'd be lucky to finish it.

None of that siege will be apparent to audiences. The Fields unction, the Fields serio-comic posturing, run through almost every foot of *Poppy*. The plot of the gay, romping insanity is about as mysterious as a cobblestone and just about as old-fashioned. No one will resent it for that. It is good antique hokum trussed up for a Fields vehicle. All that matters is that Professor Eustace McGargle is back in perfect form.

THE BIG BROADCAST OF 1938

1938

CREDITS:

Produced and distributed by Paramount. Produced by Harlan Thompson. Directed by Mitchell Leisen. Assistant director: Edward Anderson. Screenplay by Walter De Leon, Francis Martin, and Ken Englund from an adaptation by Howard Lindsay and Russel Crouse of an original story by Frederick Hazlitt Brennan. Musical direction by Boris Morros. Musical advisor: Arthur Franklin. Musical numbers and dances staged by LeRoy Prinz. Photographed by Harry Fischbeck. Art direction by Hans Dreier and Ernst Fegte. Special effects by Gordon Jennings. Sound: Gene Merritt, Don Johnson, and Charles Althouse. Film editors: Eda Warren and Chandler House. Interior decorations by A.E. Freudeman. Costumes by Edith Head. Cartoon sequence by Leon Schlesinger. Songs by Leo Robin and Ralph Rainger. "Zumi Zumi" music and lyrics by Tito Guizar, sung in Spanish by Tito Guizar. Running time: 97 minutes.

With Shirley Ross

CAST:

T. Frothingell Bellows and	
S.B. Bellows	W.C. Fields
Martha Bellows	Martha Raye
Dorothy Wyndham	Dorothy Lamour
Cleo Fielding	Shirley Ross
Scoop McPhail	Lynne Overman
Buzz Fielding	Bob Hope
Mike	Ben Blue
Bob Hayes	Lief Erikson
Grace Fielding	Grace Bradley
Turnkey	Rufe Davis
Honey Chile	Patricia Wilder
Lord Droopy	Lionel Pape
Joan Fielding	Dorothy Howe
Captain Stafford	Russell Hicks

and Billy Daniels, Michael Brooks, Jack Hubbard, Leonid Kinsky, Stanley King, Rex Moore, Bernard Punsley, Don Marion, Irving Bacon, Wally Maher, Rebecca Wassem, and James Craig

Specialty numbers by Kirsten Flagstad, Tito Guizar, and Shep Fields and his Rippling Rhythm Orchestra

SYNOPSIS:

Equipped with a powerhouse designed to pick up electric power broadcasts from short-wave radio stations and transmit that power to propellers, the S.S. *Gigantic* pulls out of New York harbor in a transatlantic race with the S.S. *Colossal*, the destination Cherbourg, France.

Buzz Fielding, radio master of ceremonies, is supposed to be aboard to supervise a daily broadcast. But when the ship pulls out, he is in jail for failing to pay alimony to three ex-wives, Cleo Fielding, Grace Fielding, and Joan Fielding.

Dorothy Wyndham, Buzz's newest lovelight, pays the alimony and Buzz and Dorothy board a speedboat to catch the ship. In jail, Buzz had revealed to his three ex-wives that he had bet on the nose of the *Gigantic* all of the money he was to receive for the broadcast. The three girls conceal themselves in the speedboat's cabin for a dual purpose—first, to prevent Buzz from marrying Dorothy; second, to collect the alimony when the ship wins.

However, the ship is owned by the brother of S.B. Bellows, who is a genius for making trouble. As millions

With Lionel Pape and Russell Hicks

of dollars are at stake, Bellows' brother directs Bellows to board the *Colossal* and delay it in order to make sure the *Gigantic* wins. When the ship departs, Bellows is setting a world record on a golf course. He plays the course on a motor scooter to save time. Finishing his game, he presses a button, the motor scooter turns into a miniature airplane and Bellows takes off—and lands on the deck of the *Gigantic*. Unaware of his mistake, he proceeds to make trouble—and plenty of it. In the meantime, Buzz and his harem arrive on the ship and Buzz takes over the job of broadcasting from Mike, who has been messing things up a little on his own account.

Looking for a place where he can cause an accident to happen, Bellows takes a group of reporters into the forbidden powerhouse on the pretense of showing them the place. Captain Stafford knows that Bellows' brother owns the ship and so shrugs his shoulders. Inside the powerhouse, Bellows nearly blows up the place and finally is

With Lionel Pape

almost electrocuted. Thoroughly frightened, he forbids Bob Hayes, the inventor, to use the contrivance.

In the meantime, Buzz is staging a magnificent radio show in the salon. The word comes that the *Colossal* is ahead of the *Gigantic* and the passengers and performers are stunned. Buzz sorrowfully tells Dorothy that unless the *Gigantic* wins he won't be able to marry her, as he will have lost all his money.

At supper he tells his ex-wives that they are out of luck for the same reason. A plot is hatched whereby Grace will lure Bellows out of the way long enough for Bob Hayes to turn on his machinery. Hayes and Dorothy Wyndham go to the powerhouse to start the machinery. He can't make it work. But the two discover that they are in love with each other.

At this point, word comes that Martha Bellows, the cockeyed daughter of Bellows, and her companion, Scoop McPhail, are at sea on a raft. Martha's fifth yacht has

just sunk under her. Bellows tells Captain Stafford to let them alone. Martha had crashed an airplane into a mirror factory, had broken nine thousand mirrors, and now was a hopeless jinx. Captain Stafford dupes Bellows and proceeds to the rescue, arriving just as the heel of Martha's shoe punctures the air-inflated rubber raft and it sinks under her and her crew. Now when Martha boards the ship, things really begin to happen. Mirrors crack; she accidentally starts the catapult whirling about the deck; and so on. The sailors go on a sit-down strike, demanding that Martha be thrown overboard; let the fish watch out for themselves. Scoop McPhail persuades the sailors

to wait until seven o'clock that evening when the seven years' bad luck runs out.

However, later, Ivan convinces the sailors that they had better not take a chance. So Martha is tossed overboard—but at that moment her bad luck runs out and she saves herself by clinging to the anchor.

Meanwhile, Bob Hayes discovers the cause of the trouble: the tip of Bellows' umbrella is wedged in the coils. This is removed and the ship leaps forward. It passes the *Colossal* and eventually wins the race. Buzz becomes reconciled with Cleo Fielding, his first ex-wife, and Dorothy Wyndham marries Bob Hayes.

With Shirley Ross and Bob Hope

REVIEWS:

Senior Scholastic

A big cast with plenty of big names, but a big disappointment, except for W.C. Fields. He goes through his act—golf and billiards—and adds a visit to a super-super filling station to bring his personal batting average near par, but the rest of the proceedings are in a bad slump. The story has to do with a transatlantic race between two streamlined liners, but most of the time, twixt here and there, is taken up with a floor show aboard the S.S. *Gigantic*. We could forgive all, but for the fact that the producers have plumped Kirsten Flagstad down in the middle of the Atlantic, as it were, and told her to sing an aria from *Die Walküre*. She sings it, and seems not to mind being one of the performers on a variety hour. We call it unfair to Wagnerian opera singers.

National Board of Review Magazine

An amusing and lavish production with most of the action taken aboard an ultramodern liner. There are good songs and the dancing is excellent.

The Daughters of the American Revolution Magazine

W.C. Fields at his funniest and Kirsten Flagstad's superb voice highlight many specialties given as a program aboard an ocean liner. A song, "Thanks for the Memories," as sung by Bob Hope, a newcomer to films, should become a hit.

YOU CAN'T CHEAT AN HONEST MAN

1939

CREDITS:

Produced and distributed by Universal. Produced by Lester Cowan. Directed by George Marshall. Assistant director: Vernon Keays. Screenplay by George Marion, Jr., Richard Mack and Everett Freeman from an original story by Charles Bogle (W.C. Fields). Musical direction by Charles Previn. Photographed by Milton Krasner. Art direction by Jack Otterson. Film editor: Otto Ludwig. Sound recording: Robert Pritchard. Running time: 76 minutes.

CAST:

Larson E. Whipsnade	W.C. Fields
Edgar Bergen	Edgar Bergen
Charlie McCarthy	Charlie McCarthy
Mortimer Snerd	Mortimer Snerd
Vicky Whipsnade	Constance Moore
Mrs. Bel-Goodie	Mary Forbes
Mr. Bel-Goodie	Thurston Hall
Princess Baba	Princess Baba
Phineas Whipsnade	John Arledge
Butler	Charles Coleman
Corbett	Edward Brophy
Burr	Arthur Hohl
Blacaman	Blacaman
Cheerful	Eddie Anderson
Chester	Grady Sutton
Deputy Sheriff	Ferris Taylor
Roger Bel-Goodie	James Bush
Ronnie	Ivan Lebedeff

With Ivan Lebedeff

SYNOPSIS:

Larson E. Whipsnade is having financial difficulty with his circus and is constantly being chased by the sheriff. To make matters worse, he can't get rid of Edgar Bergen and Charlie McCarthy because of their contract. He particularly dislikes Charlie, who is always making cracks about him.

As time passes, Charlie gripes continually because they aren't being paid. He wants Bergen to leave the circus and just about has him talked into it when Vicky Whipsnade arrives, looking for her father. Bergen immediately

falls in love with her, and Charlie sees his hopes of getting away from the circus fading.

Vicky and Bergen get along marvelously and she is beginning to fall for him. Then she discovers her father is in financial trouble and, in order to help him, she decides to marry Roger Bel-Goodie, a wealthy suitor. Roger is elated and says they will be married at his parents' home.

Bergen and McCarthy are up in a balloon when Vicky leaves the circus for her wedding. They see her and jump

With Eddie "Rochester" Anderson and Grady Sutton

with a parachute, landing right on her car. Blinded by the parachute, Vicky runs into a police car. All three of them are arrested.

Whipsnade arrives at the Bel-Goodie home for the wedding ahead of his daughter; he doesn't worry about her lateness. However, the Bel-Goodies become quite annoyed at her for being late to her own wedding.

Vicky finally arrives, gets into a terrific quarrel with Roger and his parents and says the wedding is off. She and her brother then leave with Whipsnade in his circus chariot. As they are returning to the circus, Bergen and Charlie McCarthy, who have been released from jail, overtake them on a bicycle. They return to the circus and many more problems arise. But Roger meets Vicky again and attempts to straighten out matters. Later Bergen and McCarthy are waiting in a balloon; Whipsnade quietly cuts the rope holding it to the ground. So Charlie finally gets his wish, as the balloon sails away across the sky.

REVIEWS:

Senior Scholastic

There isn't much of a story, but so many funny things happen that you're likely to overlook the lack of it. And while Mr. Fields, alias Charles Bogle, in writing the story hasn't dealt himself a very good hand, he is still a master comedian.

With Grady Sutton and Edward Brophy

Frank S. Nugent in *The New York Times*

In these days of iron ships and wooden men, it was inevitable, alas, that our old dreadnought of comedy, W.C. Fields, should be scuttled by Charlie McCarthy, the famous grandson of a whittler's mother. In this film, the great William Claude is left floundering in the verbal wake of Edgar Bergen's whispering pine. His only consolation, and it must be ours, was his choice of a new *nom de cinema*, Larson E. Whipsnade, and a portable shower bath of his own invention: an elephant called Queenie who is trained to warm the water in her trunk before spraying it fondly over her lord and master.

These are gleams of the old Fields, but they are scarcely enough to illumine a drab, labored and generally misguided comedy. Considering that he wrote it himself, Mr. Fields seems singularly ignorant of the qualities that have endeared him to his millions. His Larson E. Whipsnade, circus proprieter, is completely unsympathetic. He is a scamp, but not a loveable scamp; a blusterer who bullies for the sake of bullying and not to conceal a tender heart. Whipsnade is not the Fields we have known. We want no part of him. He is something created by the radio, the result of nagging and being nagged by a pert ventriloquist's dummy.

Charlie, possibly because the audience is on his side but more because Mr. Bergen makes him such a cute

With Edgar Bergen and Charlie McCarthy

With Constance Moore

little tyke, has all the best of the picture. At least, his material is as fresh as he is and appears to have survived editing and censoring with less damage. The Fields sequences, on the other hand, have a mutilated look. Several of them are quite pointless; others, after a promising beginning, trail off into bored slapstick. It was all most disappointing.

Frank S. Nugent in *The New York Times*

The script of *You Can't Cheat an Honest Man* is by Charles Bogle. Mr. Bogle, of course, is W.C. Fields. Mr. Fields has been having himself a time, chiefly at Charlie McCarthy's expense, at Universal. He seems to be in fine fettle, taking only the smallest nip of sherry before each shot, probably just to "refresh my recollection," as the elderly jurist once said. The day we dropped in he was doubling for Buffalo Bella, the bearded lady and trick-shot expert of the circus in an attempt to hide from the sheriff. There were five perfect takes of one gag sequence, but the first four of them were spoiled by offstage laughter. The grips, juicers, and director simply couldn't help themselves. If the rest of it is that funny, it ought to be a hilarious show.

With Edgar Bergen and Charlie McCarthy

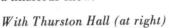

With Thurston Hall (at right)

MY LITTLE CHICKADEE

1940

With Margaret Hamilton

CREDITS:

Produced and distributed by Universal. Produced by Lester Cowan. Directed by Edward Cline. Assistant director: Joe McDonough. Original screenplay by Mae West and W.C. Fields. Musical direction by Charles Previn. Musical score by Frank Skinner. Photography by Joseph Valentine. Art direction by Jack Otterson. Film editor: Ed Curtiss. Sound supervisor: Bernard B. Brown. Gowns by Vera West. Song "Willie of the Valley," music by Ben Oakland and lyrics by Milton Drake. Running time: 83 minutes.

CAST:

Cuthbert J. Twillie	W.C. Fields
Flower Belle Lee	Mae West
Jeff Badger	Joseph Calleia
Masked Bandit	Joseph Calleia
Wayne Carter	Dick Foran
Mrs. Gideon	Margaret Hamilton
Clarence	George Moran
Old Man	Si Jenks
Bartender	James Conlin
Gene Austin	Gene Austin
Candy	Russell Hall
Coco	Otto Heimel
Henchman	Eddie Butler
Henchman	Bing Conley
Cousin Zeb	Fuzzy Knight
Miss Foster	Anne Nagel
Aunt Lou	Ruth Donnelly
Uncle John	Willard Robertson
Budge	Donald Meek
Sheriff	William B. Davidson
Judge	Addison Richards
Boy	Jackie Searle
Woman	Fay Adler
Woman	Jan Duggan
Man	Morgan Wallace
Man	Wade Boteler
Clerk	Harlan Briggs

and Jeff Conlon, John Kelly, Walter McGrail, Otto Hoffmann, Billy Benedict, Delmar Watson, Chester Gan, George Melford, Lita Chevret, Bud Harris, Bob McKenzie, James Morton, Joe Whitehead, Slim Gaut, Lloyd Ingraham, George Billings, Ben Hall, Charles McMurphy, Dick Rush, Hank Bell, Buster Slaven, Danny Jackson, Lane Chandler, Charles Hart, Jack Roper, Alan Bridge, Eddie Hearn, and Mark Anthony

With Mae West

SYNOPSIS:

Because Flower Belle Lee believes Cuthbert J. Twillie to have money, she marries him but leaves a goat with him in bed while she goes out into the hills to be enchanted by a masked lover.

During the daytime Flower attempts to teach in a local school and finds, to her surprise, that she has a class with many older men in it. She soon realizes that these men are not there for the usual schooling. Meanwhile Cuthbert, in hopes of making more money, plays in a game of cards; when he is caught cheating, he is almost hung, being saved at the last minute. There are adventures typical of the Old West, with Indians and bandits. Everything is brought to a conclusion when the bandit who has been plaguing the town is finally caught.

With George Moran

With Mae West

REVIEWS:

Newsweek

When Universal announced plans to star Mae West and W.C. Fields in a comedy, Hollywood observers tempered their admiration of a sure-fire box-office entente with concern for Edward Cline, whose position as director was expected to develop into a job of refereeing.

Fireworks were held to be inevitable not only because neither star takes kindly to a back seat, but because the comedy techniques of both are diametrically opposed. Mae West polishes her innuendos and words of wisdom with loving care and spots them in her script with the precision of a perfectionist. To Fields, on the other hand, a script is a necessary evil, to be ignored at the spur of any moment in favor of the hair-trigger ad-libbing that is the essence of his humor. But the war of temperaments failed to come off, and, if *My Little Chickadee* isn't the comedy riot it promised to be, it is hilarious enough in spots to regale admirers of the co-stars.

The West-Fields nonaggression pact was inspired in part by the fact that the two players wrote their own screen story. As literature, their burlesque fable of the Wild West of the '80s is notable chiefly for allotting both stars an equal amount of footage, and not too much of it together.

With Mae West

Mae West

With Mae West

Time

My Little Chickadee is an inspired coupling of the
suggestive art of America's leading mental strip-teaser
(Mae West) with the comic talents of one of the funniest
men on earth (W.C. Fields). Together they make a
comedy which is more hilarious than its grab-bag plot
about a fancy lady, whose efforts to roll a penniless hair-
oil salesman are insufficiently supported by good gags,
has any right to be. It also suffers less than usual from
the tendency of Comedienne West (who yearns to play
Catherine the Great) to take herself too seriously.

As highly staminate Flower Belle, Mae West spreads
her gorgeous corolla (including a butterfly bow that
coyly punctuates her posterior rhythms) in Greasewood
City, one of the West's wide-open places. There she gets
mixed up with a Masked Bandit, who turns out to be
Joseph Calleia disguised as a Cagoulard. Flower Belle's
throaty account of their first meeting: "I was in a tight
spot, but I managed to wiggle out of it." She also fakes
a marriage with Cuthbert J. Twillie (W.C. Fields) be-

With George Moran

With George Moran and Joseph Calleia

cause she thinks his bag of fake money is real, but substitutes a goat for herself in the nuptial chamber when she finds it isn't.

Not quite the box-office come-on she used to be, Miss West implements this return to her spiritual home in the gamy '90s with the expert services of Director Edward F. Cline, the ex-Keystone Cop, who invented Bathing Beauties, and Producer Lester Cowan, who taught Hollywood (with *You Can't Cheat an Honest Man*) that Comedian Fields is at his best when he is playing Comedian Fields.

Cuthbert J. Twillie is first-rate W.C. Fields clowning, which is proof enough that one of the coolest heads in show business surmounts Cinemactress West's opulent curves. For Mae, who fancies herself no end as a literatus and has always jealously insisted on authoring her own scripts, this time took a tip from Producer Cowan. She let Funnyman Fields write in his own part, ad lib to his heart's content. Best ad lib was carefully excised from the picture. Murmured Fields one day to the goat which he mistakes for Flower Belle: "Darling, have you changed your perfume?"

With Mae West and George Moran

With Mae West

With George Moran

With director Eddie Cline, doing an Edgar Bergen-Charlie McCarthy act on the set of My Little Chickadee.

With Mae West

The Times (London)

Miss Mae West and Mr. W.C. Fields are a weighty combination, but somehow or other they cannot persuade this film to run at all easily. The farcical story of the bad days in the eighties moves in a series of fits and starts and leaves the impression that the director, having thought of one passably good burlesque situation, is in a perpetual state of tearing his hair in the effort to find another. Perhaps Miss West herself is partly to blame. She has one or two effective tricks of gesture and speech, but repetition of them becomes wearisome and she has little else to fall back on. Mr. Fields is magnificently flamboyant and rhetorical in his exclamation, "What symmetrical digits," as he stoops to kiss Miss West's hand in one of the lesser flights—but hard as he works, *My Little Chickadee* obstinately refuses to gather momentum.

BANK DICK

1940

CREDITS:

Produced and distributed by Universal. Directed by Edward Cline. Original story and screenplay by Mahatma Kane Jeeves (W.C. Fields). Musical direction by Charles Previn. Photographed by Milton Krasner. Art direction by Jack Otterson. Editor: Arthur Hilton. Running time: 74 minutes.

With Jan Duggan

CAST:

Egbert Souse	W.C. Fields
Agatha Souse	Cora Witherspoon
Myrtle Souse	Una Merkel
Elsie Mae Adele Brunch Souse	Evelyn Del Rio
Mrs. Hermisillo Brunch	Jessie Ralph
J. Pinkerton Snoopington	Franklin Pangborn
Joe Guelpe	Shemp Howard
Mackley Q. Greene	Richard Purcell
Og Oggilby	Grady Sutton
J. Frothingham Waterbury	Russell Hicks
Mr. Skinner	Pierre Watkin
Filthy McNasty	Al Hill
Cozy Cochran	George Moran
Otis	Bill Wolfe
A. Pismo Clam	Jack Norton
Assistant Director	Pat West
Francois	Reed Hadley
Miss Plupp	Heather Wilde
Doctor Stall	Harlan Briggs
Mr. Cheek	Bill Alston

With Kay Sutton

With Shemp Howard

SYNOPSIS:

Some years before Egbert Souse won a Bank Night prize, and since then has done nothing more strenuous than lift a few liquid stimulants daily at the Black Pussy Cat Café.

At this same café, Egbert meets Mackley Q. Greene, manager of the Tel-Avis Picture Productions, in Souse's town (Lompoc) on a location trip. Spinning a tale of his career with Griffith, Sennett, etc., Souse impresses Greene, who engages Egbert to finish direction of a picture on which they are engaged. Egbert starts, but is called off the job when the regular director, A. Pismo Clam, sobers up.

Once more seated on a bench waiting for the Black Pussy Café to open for busines, Egbert's relaxation is spoiled when a bandit, making his escape after robbing the bank, trips over Egbert's feet. When the police arrive, Egbert is sitting on the outlaw.

At the bank, Egbert is complimented for his bravery by Mr. Skinner, the bank president, and awarded the job of special officer. While celebrating his good fortune at

With Grady Sutton (at left)

the café, Egbert meets a fast-talking stock salsman who points out the certain fortune which will come to anyone possessing a few shares in his beefsteak mine.

The proposition interests Souse, as he has a marriage-able daughter, Myrtle, who is engaged to Og Oggilby, a teller at the bank. Og can't marry on his present salary and Egbert is convinced the riches that will come to Og through the purchase of the stock will enable Og to take Myrtle off his hands.

Og agrees, and takes seven hundred dollars from the bank's funds, intending to replace it when the bank employees get their bonus in a few days. But Og and Souse find themselves in hot water when the bank examiner, J. Pinkerton Snoopington, arrives.

Souse tries to delay the bank examination by giving J. P. Snoopington a "Michael Finn," but the examiner recovers before the missing money can be replaced. Things are about to come to a disastrous climax when

With Dorothy Haas

another bandit attempts to hold up the bank. He kidnaps Souse, uses him as a shield against the bullets of the law, and forces Souse to drive the getaway car. However, Souse's manner of driving so frightens the bandit that he faints. The police arrive and arrest the bandit. Souse is again the hero of the day. He is given five thousand dollars for capturing the bandit and ten thousand dollars for the wild screen story he sells to the moving picture company. His problems are solved by the money and he now has more time to spend in the Black Pussy Cat Café.

REVIEWS:

W.R.W. in *Motion Picture Herald*

Showmen whose customers are addicted to yearning for the W.C. Fields of other years and/or the comedies that were Keystones are now in a position to promise them satisfaction of both of these yearnings in one and the same film. For here is the Fields of yore in a film of his own fashioning directed by the Edward Cline who directed more Keystones than he can remember.

Designed for humor and humor only, the Fields and Cline variety, the film seeks to entertain and do no other thing, least of all to advocate temperance.

Press-shown at the Hillstreet Theatre, Los Angeles, a cinema serving metropolitan and transient trade, where the audience laughed itself to the verge of hysterics.

Time

Bank Dick is the long-awaited reward for the followers of cob-nosed Comedian W.C. Fields. The reward is the more rewarding because his recent pictures were impeded by the disconcerting presence of irrelevant comics. In this one, the Sultan of Sloth finally achieves the kind of delightful outrage which has made his fan list long and faithful. There are 74 minutes of almost clear Fields—as much a one-man show as the fences of cinema formula will allow.

With Evelyn Del Rio

With Pierre Watkins and Fay Adler

With Evelyn Del Rio, Una Merkle, Cora Witherspoon, Jessie Ralph, and Grady Sutton

Bosley Crowther in *The New York Times*

No reflection is intended upon the appearance of W.C. Fields when we say that the great man has mellowed considerably, and for the best, since he was last among us in *My Little Chickadee*. Then he gave signs of degenerating into a pesky, cantankerous old fluff with a disposition as vile as that of a wolverine. But now, in Universal's *Bank Dick*, we welcome our old friend Bill back, as magnificently expansive as ever.

True, he is herein supported by an excellent cast of comics. But the gratifying thing is that Bill is at last given his muffin head again and is not compelled to tag along with such excess baggage as Mae West or even Charlie McCarthy. The picture belongs to him, and his name—or *nom de plume*—is stamped all over it.

To be sure, the suggestion of a story which Mahatma Kane Jeeves (or you know who) has contrived for himself is thinner than a dime and certainly no heavier. It tells of an indigent gentleman in a town called Lompoc, who accidentally captures a bandit and gets a job as bank guard in reward. Then his troubles and temptations begin and it looks as though his goose is nearly cooked, but another bank robber conveniently comes along and he again gets a chance to pull a coup.

With such a part to play around with, old Bill has the time of his life—growling, feinting, being official and forever preserving his fly-blown dignity. No one who fancies madcap comedy can reasonably afford to miss the spectacle of Bill creeping up and pouncing upon a kid with a cap-pistol in the bank; or of Bill solicitously at-

tending a bank examiner whom he has fed a "Michael Finn"; or of Bill at the wheel of the car in which a desperate bandit is attempting to escape. "The resale value of this car," says Bill from the corner of his mouth, "is going to be practically nil when we get through with this trip."

In fact, for anyone who simply likes to laugh at the reckless inanities of an inspired buffoon, we recommend *The Bank Dick*. It's great fun.

With Russell Cole

With Franklin Pangborn

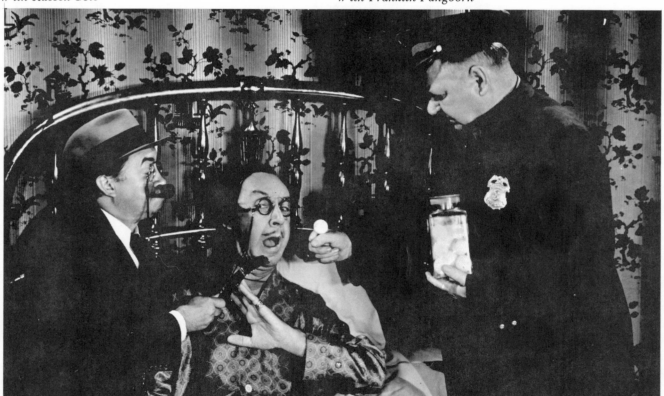

With Harlan Briggs and Franklin Pangborn

The Times (London)

Mr. W.C. Fields is magnificently independent of the material which is foisted upon him. He seems to treat the poor story and thin situations which make up this film as he treats the characters in it giving them now and again a nod of recognition, occasionally making an effort to placate them, but for the most part pushing them aside by the sheer force of his fruity, orotund personality, elbowing them into oblivion while he conducts his entranced monologues, and carries on with his own fantastic exploits in his own fantastic world.

NEVER GIVE A SUCKER AN EVEN BREAK

1941

CREDITS:

Produced and distributed by Universal. Directed by Edward Cline. Associate director: Ralph Ceder. First assistant director: Howard Christie. Assistant to Ralph Ceder: Melville Shyer. Screenplay by John T. Neville and Prescott Chaplin from an original story by Otis Criblecoblis (W.C. Fields). Musical direction by Charles Previn. Musical score by Frank Skinner. Photographed by Charles Van Enger. Cameraman: Jerome Ash. Art direction by Jack Otterson and Richard H. Riedel. Film editor: Arthur Hilton. Costumes by Vera West. Set decorations by R.A. Gausman. Sound: Bernard B. Brown. Running time: 70 minutes.

With Emil Van Horn

CAST:

The Great Man	W.C. Fields
His Niece	Gloria Jean
Butch	Billy Lenhart
Buddy	Kenneth Brown
Madame Gorgeous	Anne Nagel
The Producer	Franklin Pangborn
The Producer's Wife	Mona Barrie
The Rival	Leon Errol
Mrs. Hemogloben	Margaret Dumont
Ouliotta Hemogloben	Susan Miller
Peter Carson, a Young Engineer	Charles Lang

and Irving Bacon, Claud Allister, Leon Belasco, Emil Van Horn, Billy Wayne, Minera Urecal, Jody Gilbert, Al Hill, William Gould, Emmett Vogan, Jack Lipson, Dave Willock, Duke York, Eddie Bruce, Lloyd Ingraham, James Morton, Dick Alexander, Kay Deslys, Kathryn Sheldon, Michael Visaroff, Armand "Curley" Wright, Irene Colman, Carlotta Monti, Frank Austin, Frances Morris, Jack Roper, Emma Tansey, William Alston, Charles McMurphy, and James "Brick" Sullivan

154

With Franklin Pangborn

SYNOPSIS:

W.C. Fields goes to Esoteric Studios for a story conference, but has trouble getting there. Two candid youngsters, Butch and Buddy, inform him his latest picture is a "Buptkie," a husky gent knocks Fields into the shrubbery for eyeing the gent's girl, and a waitress drops ice water down the comedian's neck.

Fields describes a story to his producer, with little success. Wandering out, he finds his niece, Gloria Jean, playing in a shooting gallery owned by Leon Errol, father of Butch and Buddy.

Gloria's mother, Madame Gorgeous, is killed in a trapeze fall while working in a circus picture. Fields, becoming the youngster's guardian, leaves with her by airplane for Mexico where he plans to sell wooden nutmegs to members of a Russian colony there.

Fields drops a bottle out of the plane. In trying to recapture it he falls, landing on a mountaintop where live Mrs. Hemogloben, a man-eater, and her pretty daughter, Ouliotta Hemogloben. He teaches Ouliotta a kissing game, but hastily flees when Mrs. Hemogloben wants to play, too.

At the Russian colony Fields is rejoined by Gloria; he also meets Errol, Butch and Buddy, who are there ahead of him selling wooden nutmegs.

Learning from Peter Carson, an American engineer, that Mrs. Hemogloben is wealthy, Fields decides to return to the mountain and woo her.

Carson precedes Fields and woos Ouliotta. Errol likewise precedes Fields and woos Mrs. Hemogloben, so when Fields arrives he has no chance. Dejectedly he withdraws.

Then it is discovered that the whole Mexican adventure is the story Fields has been trying to sell to the producer, and which the producer does not buy.

With Franklin Pangborn and Mona Barrie

With Gloria Jean and Claude Allister

With Leon Errol

REVIEWS:

James Agee in *Time*

Never Give a Sucker an Even Break is not a movie; it is 70 minutes of photographed vaudeville by polyp-nosed W.C. Fields, assisted by Gloria Jean, Franklin Pangborn and other stage properties. As such, it is strong drink for cinemaddicts who believe that the Great Man can do no wrong, small beer for those who think that even a Fields picture should have a modicum of direction.

Sucker has no plot and needs none. It is just Fields trying to peddle a scenario to Esoteric Studios. He reads a scene, then plays it. Upshot: a maelstrom of slapstick, song, blackout, episodes, old gags, new gags, confusion. That much of it is truly comic is testimony to the fact that Comedian Fields is one of the funniest men on earth. Whether he is offering a cure for insomnia ("Get plenty of sleep"), refusing a bromo ("couldn't stand the noise"), nasally vocalizing, meticulously blowing the head off an ice cream soda, Fields is a beautifully timed exhibit of mock pomposity, puzzled ineffectualness, subtle understatement and true-blue nonchalance.

Now 62, Fields has spent most of his adult life battling babies, dogs, censors, producers, directors, the world in general. From the shape of his latest picture, it is apparent that he has Universal licked. The only round Fields is known to have lost was the production's title: he wanted it called *The Great Man*. After the present title was selected, the comedian snarled: "What does it matter; they can't get that on a marquee. It will probably boil down to *Fields—Sucker*."

Largely as a result of bickering, *Sucker* is far from being the kind of picture that only W.C. Fields could turn out. His unique talent needs intelligent direction. It does not need all the props that its owner thinks are a necessity for his performance. The great comedian can play straight better and more firmly than anyone in the business.

Otis Ferguson in *The New Republic*

There is nobody who makes bad comedies more funny than W.C. Fields—who is responsible for making them bad in the first place. *Never Give a Sucker an Even Break* is his newest and written by himself. It should have been about the life among carnival barkers and pitchmen that its title celebrates, or it should have been about something. Instead it is just an old-time farce showing Fields as a broken-down movie hack outlining a plot to a pro-

With Susan Miller and Margaret Dumont

ducer and acting out the plot through the main part of the picture. Young Gloria Jean is a sort of Deanna Durbin singer and heart interest; Fields is her uncle and although she is a cute kid I should say it generally serves her right.

There are other people scattered through the story, very scattered, and the irony of their situation is that most of what little work they do in the picture leaves you impatient for the solo appearance of the very man responsible for the dull absurdity of the state they find themselves in.

However, my sermon on the obsolescence of the movie comedy as a one-man series of turns is beginning to bore me too, and Fields of course has listened to no one since someone told him there wasn't any fire in Chicago. He is one of the natural funny men, against all odds and comers, and you could as soon reform him into pictures as you could get him on a diet of vegetable juices—probably with a result as fatal. Once again disaster is his friend; once again the forces of gravity and public opinion are against him, little recking that he is their

master, at least of ceremonies. His nose is still red but unbloody, he still finds the rich and awful widow by the middle of the picture, he has still about him that majesty of place and breeding which turns the point of any blade save his own; he is still the gay dog with the old tricks— the business with the feet, the stick, the plug hat, the reflective but sonorous aside, the topper, nasal and triumphant, with which the entire architecture of the forces for order is toppled at least once in every picture. He is usually down but he is never right, and yet there is in him a kind of humor so deeply seated that familiarity becomes somehow a further extension of our delight in this figure which is already an American legend, having built itself up by giving itself away. If there was ever a great clown in this time of changeover from beer and music hall to the universal distribution of radio and films, I would say it was in the person and the character and the undying if corny gusto of Bill Fields, who moved mountains until they fell on him, and then brushed himself off and looked around for more.

Reprinted by permission of Dorothy Chamberlain

TALES
OF
MANHATTAN

1942

With Margaret Dumont

CREDITS:

Distributed by Twentieth Century-Fox. Produced by Boris Morros and S.P. Eagle (Sam Spiegel). Directed by Julien Duvivier. Screenplay by Ben Hecht, Ferenc Molnar, Donald Ogden Stewart, Samuel Hoffenstein, Alan Campbell, Ladislas Fodor, L. Vadnai, L. Georog, Lamar Trotti and Henry Blankfort. Musical direction by Edward Paul. Original music by Sol Kaplan. Song by Leo Robbin and Ralph Rainger. Photographed by Joseph Walker. Art direction by Richard Day and Boris Leven. Film editor: Robert Bischoff. Running time: 118 minutes.

CAST:

Charles Boyer, Rita Hayworth, Ginger Rogers, Henry Fonda, Charles Laughton, Edward G. Robinson, Paul Robeson, Ethel Waters, Eddie (Rochester) Anderson, Thomas Mitchell, Eugene Pallett, Cesar Romero, Gail Patrick, Roland Young, Marion Martin, Elsa Lanchester, Victor Francen, George Sanders, James Gleason, Harry Davenport, James Rennie, J. Carrol Naish, Hall Johnson Choir, Frank Orth, Christian Rub, Sig Arno, Harry Hayden, Morris Ankrum, Don Douglas, Mae Marsh, Clarence Muse, George Reed, Cordell Hickman, Paul Renay, Barbara Lynn, Adeline DeWalt Reynolds, and Helene Reynolds

With Margaret Dumont

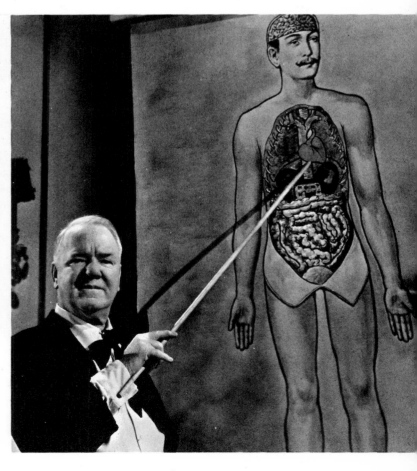

SYNOPSIS:

For this film, W.C. Fields did a twenty-minute sequence which was completely cut out of the final film because the film was too long and this sequence seemed the easiest to remove. The stills on these pages are from that sequence, which has never been shown in movie theaters.

FOLLOW THE BOYS

1944

CREDITS:

Distributed by Universal. Produced by the Charles K. Feldman Group Productions. Produced by Albert L. Rockett. Directed by Eddie Sutherland. First assistant director: Howard Christie. Original screenplay by Lou Breslow and Gertrude Purcell. Musical direction by Leigh Harline. Musical production numbers devised and staged by George Hale. Photographed by David Abel. Art direction by John B. Goodman and Harold H. MacArthur. Film editor: Fred R. Feitshans, Jr. Sound: Bernard B. Brown. Set decoration by Russell A. Gausman and Ira S. Webb. Costumes by Vera West and Howard Greer. Special effects by John P. Fulton. Running time: 118 minutes.

CAST:

Tony West	George Raft
Gloria Vance	Vera Zorina
Nick West	Charles Grapewin
Kitty	Grace MacDonald
Louie West	Charles Butterworth
Bruce	George Macready
Annie	Elizabeth Patterson
Barrett	Theodor von Eltz
Doctor Henderson	Regis Toomey
Laura	Ramsey Ames
Junior	Spooks

and Mack Gray, Molly Lamont, John Meredith, John Estes, Ralph Gardner, Doris Lloyd, Charles D. Brown, Nelson Leigh, Lane Chandler, Cyril Ring, Emmett Vogan, Addison Richards, Frank LaRue, Tony Marsh, Stanley Andrews, Leslie Denison, Leyland Hodgson, Bill Healy, Frank Jenks, Ralph Dunn, Billy Benedict, Grandon Rhodes, Howard Hickman, Edwin Stanley, Roy Darmour, Carl Vernell, Tony Hughes, Wallis Clark, Richard Crane, Frank Wilcox, Jimmy Carpenter, Bernard Thomas, Carey Harrison, George Riley, Steve Brodie, Jack Wegman, Billy Wayne, Clyde Cook, Bobby Barber, Dick Nelson, Jack Whitney, Walter Tetley, Anthony Warde, William Forrest, Tom Hanlon, Don McGill, Franklin Parker, Dennis Moore, Odessa Lauren, Nancy Brinckman, Bill Dyer, Janet Shaw, Jan Wiley, Martin Ashe, Duke York, Joel Allen, Carlyle Blackwell, Lennie Smith, Michael Kirk, Bob Ashley, Jackie Lou Harding, Genevieve Bell, Mel Schubert, Stephen Wayne, Edwin Stanley, Charles King, Don Kramer, Allan Cooke, Luis Torres, Nicnolai, John Duane, Ed Browne, Clair Freeman, Bill Meader and Eddie Kover

With Bill Wolf

THE GUEST STARS

Jeanette MacDonald, Orson Welles' Mercury Wonder Show, Marlene Dietrich, Dinah Shore, Donald O'Connor, Peggy Ryan, W.C. Fields, The Andrews Sisters, Artur Rubenstein, Carman Amaya and Her Company, Sophie Tucker, Delta Rhythm Boys, Leonard Gautier's Bricklayers, Ted Lewis and His Band, Freddie Slack and His Orchestra, Charlie Spivak and His Orchestra, Louis Jordan and His Orchestra, Louise Beavers, Clarence Muse, Maxie Rosenbloom, Maria Montez, Susanna Foster, Louise Allbritton, Robert Paige, Alan Curtis, Lon Chaney, Gloria Jean, Andy Devine, Turhan Bey, Evelyn Ankers, Noah Beery Jr., Gale Sondergaard, Peter Coe, Nigel Bruce, Thomas Gomez, and Sam Hinds

SYNOPSIS:

The story begins on the night big-time vaudeville made its last stand at the Palace Theater in New York City. On the closing bill is a dancing act called "The Three Wests." After vaudeville folded, the Wests obtain a burlesque booking, then Tony decides to stake everything on a fling at Hollywood. As a chorus boy in a film musical, he calls attention to himself by criticizing the dancing star. His temerity leads to his elevation as her partner; they are co-starred, and later they marry.

Refused for physical reasons when he tries to enlist in the Army after Pearl Harbor, Tony becomes one of the hard-working organizers of the Hollywood Victory Committee. Through marital misunderstandings which cause Gloria to leave him, Tony carries on to launch the parade of stars who entertain the Armed Services he was not permitted to join.

REVIEWS:

Frank L. Moore in *The Hollywood Citizen-News*

It's a good picture in spite of itself. *Follow the Boys* is a jumble of variety acts wrapped up with an unbelievable plot. The acts, however, are individually so good that they lift the film solidly into the first-rate entertainment class.

Ed Sullivan in *The Hollywood Citizen-News*

What matters is the fact that the top performers are on hand to do their stuff. When you see W.C. Fields running through his elliptical billiard cue routine before a group of inductees, for example, there is no question that *Follow the Boys* is in the great tradition of showmanship.

With director Edward Sutherland between scenes of Follow the Boys

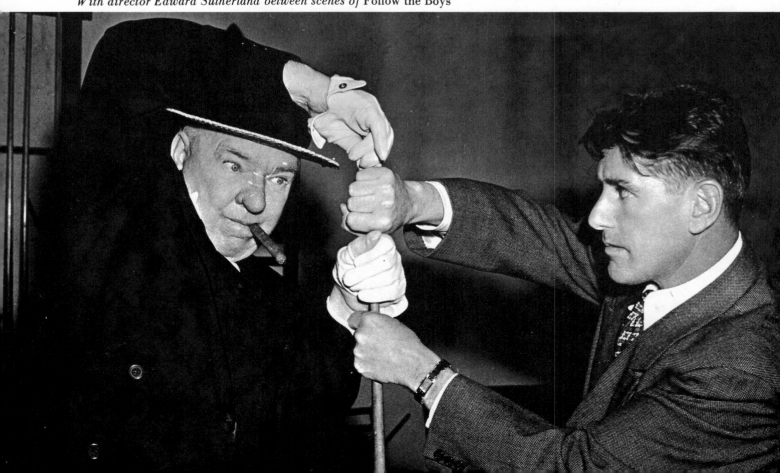

With Bill Wolf

The New York Times

Mr. Fields' appearance in *Follow the Boys* is a brief one, devoted chiefly to his often described, but seldom seen, pool table burlesque. In the picture Fields uses the same trick pool table he employed on the big variety circuit all over the world and in the Follies. He bought it in 1903 in a Birmingham, England, billiard salon and then had it rebuilt for gags by a vaudeville prop firm. The table is so constructed that, if the balls are racked on one side of the spot, a cue ball, driven into the apex of the triangle, will knock every one of them off the table. Racked an inch to another side of the spot, the cut ball will send all the others into the pockets. There is a place on the table where the grotesquely twisted cues used by Fields can be thrust right through to the floor in a comedy master stroke.

James Agee in *Time*

W.C. Fields, looking worn-and-torn but noble as Stone Mountain, macerates a boozy song around his cigar butt and puts on his achingly funny pool exhibition with warped cues.

SONG OF THE OPEN ROAD

1944

CREDITS:

Distributed by United Artists. Produced by Charles R. Rogers. Assistant to the producer: William J. Fender. Directed by S. Sylvan Simon. Assistant directors: Maurie Suess and Phil Carlstein. Screenplay by Albert Mannheimer from an unpublished story by Irving Phillips and Edward Verdier. Musical direction by Charles Previn. Music by Walter Kent; lyrics by Kim Gannon. Musical presentations by George Dobbs. Photographed by John W. Boyle. Art direction by Bernard Herzbrun. Film editor: Truman K. Wood. Production manager: Val Paul. Running time: 93 minutes.

CAST:

Charlie McCarthy	Charlie McCarthy
Edgar Bergen	Edgar Bergen
Jane Powell	Jane Powell
W.C. Fields	W.C. Fields
Bonnie	Bonita Granville
Peggy	Peggy O'Neill
Jack	Jackie Moran
Bill	Bill Christy
Director Curtis	Reginald Denny
Connors	Regis Toomey
Mrs. Powell	Rose Hobart
Spolo	Sig Arno
Miss Casper	Irene Tedro
Pat Starling	Pat Starling

and Sammy Kaye and His Orchestra. Specialty numbers by The Condon Brothers, Hollywood Canteen Kids, Lipham Four, Chuck Faulkner Band, and Catron and Pop

SYNOPSIS:

Miss Powell is a child movie star, successful but lonely, who, after making a picture about the CCC with a group of young pickers, longs to rejoin their nomad life. In fact, she gleefully ditches her next plum role, leaves Mama a farewell note, and bicycles off to help harvest a tomato crop about to perish for lack of pickers.

Having dyed her hair, acquired a new hairdo, and changed her name from Powell to Price, the young lady can enjoy ham and eggs with the gang unrecognized. But, worse luck, she fancies herself not only something of a mechanic, but an adolescent Cupid, ruins half a dozen good bicycles, and nearly spoils two perfectly good romances. So everybody picks tomatoes but Jane, who by this time is a sad case of social ostracism. When disaster befalls these youthful farmers, our heroine dashes back to Hollywood to save the day by bringing back members of the movie colony to help save the crop.

With Jane Powell

REVIEWS:

The New York Times

Song of the Open Road, which came to Loew's Criterion yesterday, introduces to the screen Jane Powell, a winsome youngster with a prematurely developed rich soprano voice. The picture also introduces what certainly must be a new high in adolescent insipidity. At such times as the children can be, in a manner of speaking, sent out of the scene, Edgar Bergen–Charlie McCarthy, W.C. Fields and other name acts are slid in to bring the picture up to something approaching acceptable adult entertainment. But even with that, about the best that can be said for the Charles R. Rogers production is that it brings to the screen a young lady with artistic promise.

Alton Cook in *The New York World-Telegram*

The main thing to watch for in *Song of the Open Road* is its introduction of a new singing girl who seems certain to become a star in her next picture or two. Certain that is, unless she gets another picture as much below par as this current film. She gets in bad by her blunders, but she squares things with the other kids by summoning Sammy Kaye's Orchestra, Charlie McCarthy and W.C. Fields. Getting those people into the picture squares things with the audience a little too. They get little enough aside from that. A clue to the care not lavished on the film, though, is the impression that the Charlie McCarthy–W.C. Fields sequence is not nearly so good as some of their radio exchanges.

John McManus in *PM*

The resumption of the Fields–McCarthy feud, incidentally, shows W.C. happily back in his old hearty fighting form. Charlie McCarthy wins the argument, as usual, this time with an unexpected ally: Charlie McCarthy, Jr., no less.

With Edgar Bergen and Charlie McCarthy

SENSATIONS OF 1945

1944

CREDITS:

Distributed by United Artists. Produced and directed by Andrew L. Stone. Assistant to Mr. Stone: Carley Harriman. Assistant producer: James Nasser. First assistant director: Henry Kesler. Screenplay by Dorothy Bennett from an original story by Frederick Jackson and Andrew Stone. Musical direction by Mahlon Merrick. Photographed by Peverell Marley and John Mescall. Art direction by Charles Odds. Film editor: Jimmy Smith. Dance director: David Lichine. Music by Al Sherman. Lyrics by Harry Tobias. Interior decorations: Maurice Yates. Acrobatics director: Charles O'Curran. Running time: 87 minutes.

CAST:

Ginny Walker	Eleanor Powell
Junior Crane	Dennis O'Keefe
Dan Lindsey	C. Aubrey Smith
Gus Crane	Eugene Pallette
Julia Westcott	Mimi Forsythe
Randall	Lyle Talbot
The Great Gustafson	Hubert Castle
Himself	W.C. Fields
Herself	Sophie Tucker
Herself	Dorothy Donegan
Themselves	The Christianis
Themselves	Pallenberg Bears
Themselves	Cab Calloway and His Band
Themselves	Woody Herman and His Band

Himself	David Lichine
Pendergast	Richard Hageman
Miss Grear	Marie Blake
Mr. Collins	Stanley Andrews
Himself	"Uncle Willie"
Himself	Gene Rodgers
Himself	Mel Hall
Themselves	Johnson Brothers
Themselves	Flying Copelands
Themselves	Les Paul Trio

and Louise Currie, Betty Wells, Bert Roch, Grandon Rhodes, Earl Hodgings, Constance Purdy, Joe Devlin, George Humbert, Wendell Niles, Anthony Warde, Ruth Lee, and Willie Pratt

SYNOPSIS:

A super-publicity agency that specializes in the sensational is managed by a father and son. The old man will deal with any act but the son is ultraconservative. In order to cure the boy of his safe and sane ways, Pappy turns over the reins temporarily to a dancer-client. The stunts she devises are high powered, but when the lady stubs her toe, sonny boy is the one who rushes to the rescue.

ANDREW STONE'S

SENSATIONS

starring

ELEANOR P

WITH

DENNIS O'KEEFE · W

With C. Aubrey Smith, Eleanor Powell, and Dennis O'Keefe

REVIEWS:

Dorothy Manners in *The Los Angeles Examiner*

A super-vaudeville show strung along an ingenuous and unusual plot is *Sensations of 1945*. It hits the mark in every department. Eleanor Powell, long missing from the screen, is at her tap-dancing best. Dennis O'Keefe falls heir to that rarity of rarities in musicals, a good acting role. The "specialties" are lavish and gay.

Peggy Harford in *The Hollywod Citizen-News*

Sensations of 1945 brings Eleanor Powell back to the screen after a long absence, in an Andrew Stone production notable for its spectacular dance sequences.

Otherwise the picture is just another one of the epidemic of musicals, loaded with specialties, which have been sneaking up on box offices everywhere lately. The music is strictly "jive" and no song emerges melodious enough to remember.

MORE
ABOUT
FIELDS

THE OLD-FASHIONED WAY

by Otis Ferguson

Woolchester Cowperthwaite Fields is among the great one-man shows. He has been able to write his name in lights since before the incandescent bulb was invented, and within his own special province he is still the funniest fraud who ever pitched them into the aisles from laughter. He started with a line of chatter and some balls and cigar boxes, which he juggled with a snore of comment and defiance of the laws of gravity, which quickly established him as a character, which character he gradually filled out to the full limits of burlesque and vaudeville and Follies skits. Since then the movies were invented and a form for them gradually developed. But nobody told him about the new invention; nobody was able. He made movie shorts of course, and they were wonderful; he did skits in feature pictures and they were wonderful too. But movies as something different he never heard of. They grew up and he never found out which shell the pea was under, because he couldn't be bothered: that was just a rival pitch. This way, folks, test your skill, etc.

Biographers of The Incomparable, the Marvel of the Aged in Wood, will, I am sure, find it in the record that he was not only a bad boy in school but they had to change the numbers on the rooms to get him from one grade to the other. And that when he was kidnaped from upper third at the age of fourteen by a passing minstrel show he was already very unruly and set in his ways.

That learning was the other fellow's game, and being a born pitch-man he would never be a sucker for it; but that when he played he played for keeps. That when movies came along he took a look at his first camera and said, Why I can lick that, easiest thing in the world, yes— did you note what I did to them at the Palace by any chance? (You did, eh. . . .) And that even after he got himself blackballed in every producer's office on the Coast, his firm belief was that any wheeze routine could be extended by gags and names like Throttlebottom to what the rest of the world was beginning to know as a modern film comedy.

He still believes it. His new movie was written by him and mostly directed by him and then stolen by him in the principal part. It is called *Bank Dick* and it shows Fields in the uniform of a detective and all-around door man for the local bank (he was given the job as a reward, under the severest misapprehension). He gets into trouble as nobody else can, and gets out the same way; he is the harried man of family and emperor of the world, his address and resource are infinite except when approaching a simple flight of steps, he is fastidious to the high point of using his chaser for a finger bowl, he is dignity with a red nose, and courtly, and he has never truckled to any man, which would naturally not include small boys and his own shadow—which if it ever moves back a step he will make like he is going to wring its

neck. He is W.C. Fields, which is a considerable sort of thing to be, and purely a joy to watch. But that is all the movie is about.

When the man is funny he is terrific, but in between the high points—and they are as good in stage device as in line and in character conception—what is the audience doing? The story is makeshift, the other characters are stock types, the only pace discernible is in the distance between drinks or the rhythm of the fleeting seconds it takes Fields to size up trouble coming and duck to hell out. The audience is asleep because this was never made as a picture. It is stiff and static and holds no interest outside of W.C. Fields—you don't care what happens to anybody else, you don't care what the outcome; you forget immediately if there was any. Today there are no one-man shows in good pictures, unless the man is a director, and even then he must have a script and people to work with. Today we ask that even such a genius of character act as W.C. Fields be built-in, and that the structure as a whole amount to something, however light or little.

I hoped once that he would some day be content not to run the whole show in his own way, and let someone write him into and direct him through a story infinitely more absorbing than anything he has ever done. It would be the story of one of the world's deathless fools, a snide and bulbous sort of man who knew the top from the bottom, having been on both; a man who could make a comeback and throw it away and make another, a man getting old and very sick, and still coming back to damn all and do it his way, with his legs weak and his face changed to puffy, still talking through his nose like a bugle and still touching here and there the springs of human laughter. In this dream story you could even call the character Throttlebottom, though we would know who he is; and though we don't know the end, you could make one that would bring home not only what a joy he has been, to the hearts of his countrymen, but how dear. The end would be that he made a picture called *Bank Dick* in which he was a good part of his old and indomitable self, and which he was fully himself in writing, directing, acting and atmosphering in the face of almost everything that ever happened in the movies. He was W.C. Fields in it, the trouper of all troupers once again.

From *The New Republic*, December 30, 1940. Reprinted by permission of Dorothy Chamberlain.

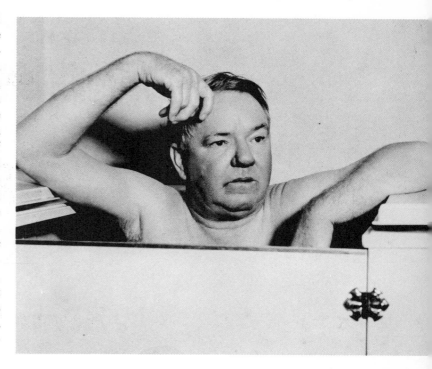

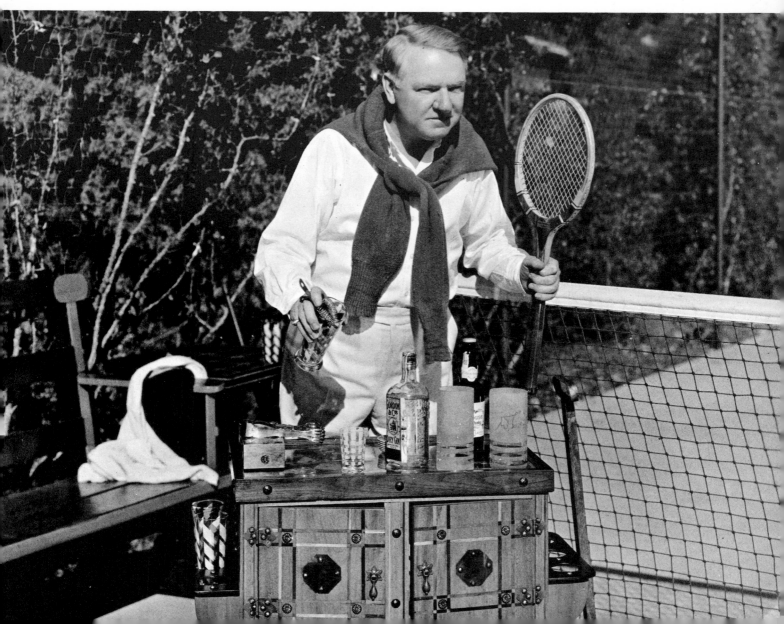

W. C. FIELDS AND THE COSMOS

by Heywood Broun

To me this seems a year in which the musical comedies distinctly show the way to so-called legitimate attractions. My quarrel with that word "legitimate" is deep and of long standing. I have never been able to understand why entertainment becomes more important simply because no one sings. In recent years I begin to sense a new point of view among critics. When I held a reviewer's post on a morning paper, it was practically treason not to choose a comedy or a farce if it happened to open on the same night as a musical show. Now there are heretics who abandon the old principle. It would be folly to do otherwise.

For instance, there came a night not so long ago in which the choice lay between W.C. Fields in *Ballyhoo* at the Hammerstein's Theater and a comedy drama entitled *Life Is Like That*. Some few of the pundits insisted on being faithful to the memory of Shakespeare and passed up Mr. Fields to witness *Life Is Like That*. The loss was theirs. I found Fields to be at the very top of his glorious best, and I liked the story in which he is set.

A satire on C.C. Pyle, the sporting promoter, has long seemed one of the neglected spaces in the American drama. I will not maintain that the plot runs down all

With Mae West and N.J. Blumberg, president of Universal Pictures, in 1940

the possibilities of the subject matter. But, at least, the scheme endows Fields with a role in which he is believable as well as amusing.

It is well to remember that a performance in musical comedy is a piece of acting just as a portrayal of Hamlet, the Prince of Denmark, may be. I will grant that there are depths and subtleties in *Hamlet* not likely to be found in the usual revue. On the other hand, low comedy parts are vastly better played in most instances. I do not see why any sensitive connoisseur of acting should not vastly prefer W.C. Fields to Walter Hampden. A good comic moves in a plane high above the head of an indifferent tragedian. It might be an excellent idea for the American public to pause in its continual program of self-reproach and take a little pride in the fact that we lead the world in the matter of musical comedy.

Ballyhoo is not a perfect specimen, but it is amply excellent to provide a hilarious evening. Several of the regular critics found it dull, but I think they are too captious and to some extent it is the custom to remain slightly aloof and calm while writing about revues.

Much is made of the fact that Mr. Fields does things now which he has shown us previously. This seems to me an ungrateful form of criticism. The fact that he can produce endless fun by capers in an Austin car should not be minimized simply because some seasons ago he did tricks with a Ford. And I feel that one of the high spots in the present theatrical year has been underlined in red because W.C. Fields is juggling again.

I am of the opinion that in this diversion the man falls little short of genius. You may protest that juggling does not belong among the major arts. Such an opinion will be held only by those who have witnessed merely the proficient practitioners. Fields is, as far as I know, the only one who is able to introduce the tragic note in the handling of a dozen cigar boxes. When they are pyramided, only to crash because of a sudden off-stage noise, my heart goes out to the protagonist as it seldom does to Lear or Macbeth.

If one thinks of art in terms of line and movement then I suggest that there is present in this juggling act as much to please the eye as when Pavlova dances. Like the best of modern painters, Fields can afford to depart from the orthodox because he is heretical from choice and not through incapacity. I mean, it is amusing when he muffs a trick because you know that he could easily complete

it if he cared to. Certainly, there is something admirable in the ability to emotionalize the task of tossing spheres into the air and catching them in rhythm. Possibly there is even profundity in such a pastime.

Mr. Fields at play among the planets suggests to me an Einsteinian quality. I do not like to rush into symbolism, but if a mortal can personally see to it that these complicated orbits are preserved, each in its entity, then I go home more sure of the safety and sanctity of the universe than before.

And yet, it might be simpler merely to say that *Ballyhoo* is excellent entertainment.

From *The Nation*, January 7, 1931

INDEX

INDEX

Agee, James, 158, 169
Alden, Mary, 50, 51, 52, 62
Alice in Wonderland, 25, 86–88
Allan, Elizabeth, 106
Allen, Gracie, 80, 81, 82, 89, 90
Allen, Judith, 95, 96
Ames, Adrienne, 92, 94
Anderson, Eddie (Rochester), 134, 135, 162

Bakshy, Alexander, 69–70, 75
Bank Dick, 17, 25, 148–153, 180–183
Barber Shop, The, 78
Barrymore, John, 30
Barrymore, Lionel, 30, 106
Bartholomew, Freddie, 106, 107, 108, 109, 110
Bates, Granville, 121, 123, 126
Beaudine, William, 95
Bennett, Joan, 25, 112, 113, 114
Bennett, Richard, 73
Bergen, Edgar, 25, 134, 137, 139, 170, 172, 173
Bernhardt, Sarah, 22
Big Broadcast of 1938, The, 25, 128–133
Blane, Sally, 62, 64
Blue, Ben, 128
Bogle, Charles, 29, 95, 103, 117, 134, 139
Boland, Mary, 73, 89, 90
Brennan, Walter, 117
Brian, Mary, 53, 54, 55, 56, 57, 117, 118, 119
Brooks, Louise, 44, 45
Broun, Heywood, 23, 184–187
Bruckman, Clyde, 76, 117
Burns, George, 80, 81, 82, 89, 90

Cadell, Jean, 106, 107, 108, 109
Calleia, Joseph, 140, 144, 145
Carter, Louise, 92
Cavanna, Elise, 78, 92
Cecil, Nora, 92, 95, 121
Chaplin, Charles, 22
Chevalier, Maurice, 22
Christie Studios, 59
Cline, Edward, 69, 140, 142, 145, 146, 148, 151, 154

Cooke, Alistair, 123–24
Cooper, Gary, 73, 86, 87, 88
Conklin, Chester, 56, 58, 59, 60, 61, 62, 64, 65
Cowan, Lester, 25, 134, 140, 145
Crabbe, Larry "Buster," 92, 93
Cromwell, Richard, 121
Crosby, Bing, 25, 112, 113, 114, 116
Crouse, Russell, 128
Crowther, Bosley, 152
Cruze, James, 73
Cukor, George, 106

David Copperfield, 25, 106–111
Davies, Marion, 23, 36, 37
Dee, Frances, 73
Del Rio, Evelyn, 148, 151, 152
Dempster, Carol, 24, 38, 39, 40, 41
Dentist, The, 76
Donnelly, Dorothy, 23, 38, 121
Doucet, Catherine, 121, 123, 124, 125
Duggan, Jan, 95, 112, 140, 148
Dukenfield, Claude William (W. C. Fields), 17, 19
Dukenfield, James, 19
Dumont, Margaret, 154, 161, 162, 163
Duvivier, Julian, 162

Ebuerne, Maude, 65, 121
Edward VII, King, 21–2
Erikson, Lief, 128
Errol, Leon, 65, 68, 86, 154, 156, 158
Erwin, Stuart, 80, 82
Evans, Madge, 106

Fatal Glass of Beer, 76–77
Fazenda, Louise, 59, 60, 61, 86
Felton, Kate, 19
Ferguson, Otis, 9, 101, 158–161, 180—183
Fields, Shep, 128
Flagstad, Kirsten, 128, 133
Follow the Boys, 25, 29, 164–65
Fools for Luck, 62–3
Ford, Harrison, 36, 41

Gallagher, "Skeets," 50, 51, 86
George White's Scandals, 23

Gilbert, Billy, 69
Golf Specialist, The, 64
Grant, Cary, 86
Granville, Bonita, 170
Griffith, D.W., 23–4, 38, 40, 41, 43

Ham Tree, The, 22
Hall, Mordaunt, 46, 49, 51–52, 64, 84
Hamilton, Margaret, 140
Hart, Lorenz, 112
Hecht, Ben, 162
Henderson, Del, 92, 95, 99, 103, 121
Henry, Charlotte, 86, 88
Herbert, Hugh, 69
Her Majesty Love, 65–68
Holloway, Sterling, 80, 86
Hope, Bob, 128, 132, 133
Hopper, E. Mason, 36
Horton, Edward Everett, 86
Houdini, Harry, 24
Howard, Kathleen, 92, 103, 117, 118, 119, 120
Hudson, Rochelle, 121, 125, 126
Hughes, Harriet (Mrs. W.C. Fields), 22
Humberstone, H. Bruce, 73

If I Had a Million, 18, 72–75
International House, 25, 80–82
Irving, George, 56, 92
Irwin, Fred, 21, 184
It's a Gift, 103–105
It's the Old Army Game, 44–6

Janice Meredith, 23, 36–7
Jean, Gloria, 154, 157, 158, 161, 165
Joyce, Alice, 47
Joyce, Peggy Hopkins, 80, 81, 82

Kane, Babe, 76, 78
Karns, Roscoe, 73, 86
Kennedy, Tom, 59, 121
Kenton, Earl, 92
Kirkwood, James, 41
Krasner, Milton, 134, 148

La Cava, Gregory, 47, 49, 53
Lamour, Dorothy, 128
Lanchester, Elsa, 106, 108, 162
Lasky, Jessie, 44
Laughton, Charles, 73, 111, 162
Lawton, Frank, 106, 108, 109, 110, 111
LeBaron, William, 95, 103, 117, 121
Leisen, Mitchell, 128
LeRoy, Baby, 17, 28, 83, 86, 87, 95, 96, 97, 98, 103
Lewis, Vera, 117
Lindsay, Howard, 128
Littlefield, Lucien, 73, 74, 86, 117
Lloyd, Harold, 31
Lord, Pauline, 99, 101, 102
Lubitsch, Ernst, 73
Luden, Jack, 56, 62
Lugosi, Bela, 80
Lunt, Alfred, 38, 39
Lyon, Ben, 65, 66, 68

McCarey, Leo, 89
McCarthy, Charlie, 18, 25, 134, 137, 139, 170, 172, 173
McEvoy, J.P., 44, 50, 51, 92, 103
McLeod, Norman, 73, 86, 103
Madison, Julian, 103
Man on the Flying Trapeze, The 117–120
Mankiewicz, Joseph L., 69, 73, 86
Manners, Dorothy, 177
Marsh, Joan, 92, 93
Marsh, Mae, 86, 162
Marshall, George, 134
Martin, Francis, 80, 83, 112, 128
Meek, Donald, 99, 140
Merkel, Una, 148, 152
Miller, Marilyn, 65, 66, 67, 68
Miller, Susan, 154, 161
Million Dollar Legs, 69–71
Mississippi, 18, 25, 112–116
Mitchell, Thomas, 17, 162
Mix, Tom, 22
Monti, Charlotte, 154
Moore, Constance, 134, 138
Mrs. Wiggs of the Cabbage Patch, 99–102
My Little Chickadee, 140–147, 152

Nagel, Anne, 140, 154
Never Give a Sucker an Even Break, 25, 154–161
Newmeyer, Fred, 50, 51
Nugent, Frank, 137, 138

Oakie, Jack, 24, 69, 71, 73, 86, 87, 88
O'Connor, Una, 106
O'Keefe, Dennis, 174, 177
Old-Fashioned Way, 95–98, 180–183
Oliver, Edna May, 86, 87, 88, 106, 110
O'Sullivan, Maureen, 106
Overman, Lynn, 121, 122, 123, 128

Pallette, Eugene, 174
Pangborn, Franklin, 80, 148, 153, 154, 155, 157, 158
Pasadena, Calif., 25
Patrick, Gail, 112, 113, 162
Pawle, Lennox, 106
Pawley, Ed, 112
Pearce, Leslie, 76
Pharmacist, The, 78
Philadelphia, Pa., 19, 22
Pitts, Zasu, 99, 100, 101, 102
Pool Sharks, 23, 24, 35
Poppy, 18, 23–24, 31, 121–127
Potters, The, 50–52
Powell, Eleanor, 174, 177
Powell, Jane, 170, 172, 177
Power, Tyrone, 36
Previn, Charles, 140, 148, 154, 170

Raft, George, 73
Rainger, Ralph, 80, 89, 121, 128, 162
Ralph, Jessie, 106, 148, 152
Rathbone, Basil, 106
Raye, Martha, 128
Raymond, Gene, 73
Reisner, Charles F., 62
Ripley, Arthur, 78
Roberts, Stephen, 73
Robin, Leo, 80, 121, 128, 162
Robson, May, 73, 86, 87
Rodgers, Richard, 112
Rogers, Buddy, 50, 116
Rogers, Will, 22
Ross, Shirley, 25, 128, 132
Rouverol, Jean, 103, 112
Ruggles, Charles, 73, 86, 89, 90
Running Wild, 53–55
Sally of the Sawdust, 24, 38–40
Seiter, William, 73
Selznick, David O., 106
Sennett, Mack, 76–79
Sennwald, Andre, 11, 97, 102, 104, 116
Sensations of 1945, 174–177
Shaw, George Bernard, 125

Simon, S. Sylvan, 170
Six of a Kind, 89–91
Skipworth, Alison, 72–75, 83–84, 86, 88, 89, 90
Smith, C. Aubrey, 174, 177
Song of the Open Road, 170–173
So's Your Old Man, 47–49
Spiegel, Sam, 162
Stone, Andrew, 174, 177
Stone, Lewis, 106
Sullivan, Ed, 168
Sutherland, Edward, 24, 44, 59, 80, 112, 121, 125, 149, 164, 168
Sutton, Grady, 78, 117, 134, 135, 137, 148, 152
Swain, Mack, 59
Swanson, Gloria, 31

Tales of Manhattan, 162–163
Taurog, Norman, 73, 99, 101
Taylor, Deems, 36
Taylor, Kent, 99
That Royle Girl, 24, 40–43
Tillie and Gus, 83–85
Tillie's Punctured Romance, 59–61
Tiomkin, Dimitri, 86
Troy, William, 82, 108
Tucker, Sophie, 174
Turpin, Ben, 69
Two Flaming Youths, 56–58
Twyman, Alan P., 13

Vallee, Rudy, 25, 80
Venable, Evelyn, 99
Vorkapich, Slavko, 106

Walpole, Hugh, 106, 108, 110
Waters, John, 56, 58
Wells, Jacqueline, 83, 86
West, Mae, 140, 141, 142, 143, 144, 145, 146, 147, 186
Witherspoon, Cora, 148, 152
Wynn, Ed, 30

You Can't Cheat an Honest Man, 134–139, 145
Young, Roland, 106, 108, 110, 111, 162
Young, Tammany, 89, 92, 95, 103, 117, 121
You're Telling Me, 31, 92–94

Ziegfeld, Flo, 23, 30
Ziegfeld Follies, 23, 30, 76
Zorina, Vera, 164
Zukor, Adolph, 25, 44